ACCIDENTS IN NORTH AMERICAN MOUNTAINEERING

VOLUME 7 • NUMBER 4 • ISSUE 52

1999

THE AMERICAN ALPINE CLUB
GOLDEN

THE ALPINE CLUB OF CANADA
BANFF

ISSN 0065-082X

ISBN # 0-930410-85-8

Manufactured in the United States of America

Published by
The American Alpine Club, Inc.
710 Tenth Street, Suite 100
Golden, CO 80401

Cover Photo
Members of the Mountain Rescue Association (MRA) practice crevasse rescue techniques on Mount Hood during the 40th Anniversary of the MRA in 1998. A volunteer organization dedicated to saving lives through rescue and mountain safety education, the MRA was founded in Washington in 1958 and held its first official meeting at Timberline Lodge in 1959. (Photograph by Charley Shimanski, Executive Director, American Alpine Club)

♻ Printed on recycled paper

CONTENTS

SAFETY COMMITTEES 1998

The American Alpine Club

Aram Attarian, John Dill, Jeff Fongemie, Mike Gauthier, Jeff Sheetz, James Yester, and John E. (Jed) Williamson *(Chairman)*

The Alpine Club of Canada

Helmut Microys, Murray Toft, and Rod Plasman *(Chairman)*

ACCIDENTS IN
NORTH AMERICAN MOUNTAINEERING

Fifty-Second Annual Report of the Safety Committees
of The American Alpine Club and The Alpine Club of Canada

Canada: I would like to start by thanking Geoff Powter for compiling the Canadian incidents for the 1998 edition. He took this project on in addition to his good work in editing the *Canadian Alpine Journal*. There were fewer accidents in 1998 than in previous years. Part of this can be attributed to the fabulous summer weather that prevailed in all of Western Canada. Many traditional snow and ice routes changed markedly, or even disappeared under the warm summer sun. There is no way of telling how many folks were out climbing last summer, but it is safe to say there were many more than usual, all taking advantage of the beautiful conditions. If this assumption is true, the percentage of accidents per climber days would definitely be down.

As Geoff reported last year, the increase in the number of ice climbing accidents is continuing. We are seeing ice climbers with lots of technical ability, but with very little "mountain sense." It will be interesting to see if this is a trend.

The number of incidents of "stranded" climbers continues to be an issue, and is mostly attributable to inexperience.

I would like to thank all of the contributors, including: Tim Auger, Marc Ledwidge, J.P. Cors, Sylvai Forrest, and George Field.

United States: We know that everything goes in cycles. In the case of mountaineering accidents, just when we think a certain kind of cause is under control, in comes an unusual number of reports on that category. It will be obvious that there were too many lowering and rappelling incidents in which anchors were inadequate or the ropes were "too short," resulting in rapid descents to the ground. (In one incident, the victim stated, "The ground acted as an effective brake.")

In catching up on accidents from Eldorado Canyon State Park from the previous year, I learned that, according to Tim Metzger (with the Division of Parks), of the 250,000 visitors per year, 100,000 of those are technical rock climbers. The trick now is to figure out how many of them are repeat visitors, given the high concentration of climbers in the area. A reasonable and conservative estimate would be 5–10,000, leaving few who would be one-time visitors. As there are guides and climbing classes conducted by schools and programs, another aspect to determine is how many of the technical climbers are just clients for a day. In any case, Eldorado Canyon is certainly one of the most heavily used areas in the state.

Mount Hood and Mount Rainier receive a lot of publicity, especially when a major incident occurs. Fifty years ago, there were only a couple of hundred attempts per year on each, and now there are over 10,000. On Mount Rainier, the summit success rate is fifty percent. In the hundred or so years that records have been kept, Mount Hood has seen well over a hundred fatalities, while the count on Mount Rainier is just under 100. Last summer, each mountain experienced a big avalanche event, resulting in two fatalities. Descriptions will be found in the narrative section. An important thing to remember about avalanches is that 90 percent of them are triggered by the individuals who die in them. In Washington, avalanches have resulted in the deaths of 180 people— more than for any other natural phenomena in the state.

In the aftermath of these events, one reporter ventured that most "world-class" (whatever is meant by that is not explained) climbers "are dead before they are 40." I would respectfully dispute that statement, and suggest that a look at data, even from Himalayan climbing, would show this statement to be at the least misleading. The reason the American Alpine Club continues to produce this report is to provide enough data to determine whether a large ("most"), moderate, or small percentage of climbers—experienced ("world-class") or otherwise—meet an early demise. Given a conservative estimate of 300 to 500,000 active climbers and an average of 27 fatalities per year in the United States for the past ten years, which includes *anyone* who died in a climbing accident, suggests that reporters need to familiarize themselves with the facts.

A big, on-going discussion that got a lot of press again this year is whether individuals who need to be rescued should be charged for these services. This is a "stay tuned" issue, especially with politicians becoming involved and suggesting legislation to address what is perceived by them as a significant burden upon the tax payers. Fortunately, at least so far, the facts about actual costs of mountain rescue versus other kinds of rescue operations are coming into focus. One sensational and seemingly costly mountain rescue can obscure the vastly greater amounts spent on lost hikers or boaters. The bottom line is this: SAR (Search and Rescue) costs for climbers are about six to eight percent of the total for this activity in our federal lands system.

In addition to the Safety Committee, we are grateful to the following (with apologies for any omissions) for collecting data and helping with the report: Hank Alicandri, Micki Canfield, Jim Detterline, George Hurley, Renny Jackson, Mark Magnuson, Daryl Miller, Leo Paik, James Roberts, Robert Speik, Ian Wade, and, of course, George Sainsbury.

John E. (Jed) Williamson
Managing Editor
7 River Ridge Road
Hanover, NH 03755
e-mail: jedwmsn@sover.net

Rod Plasman
Canadian Editor
132 Settler Way
Canmore, AB T1W 1E2
e-mail: rod.plasman@town.banff.ab.ca

CANADA

STRANDED, DARKNESS, INEXPERIENCE
Alberta, Rocky Mountains, Weeping Wall

On March 7 at 2200, Jasper wardens received a report of stranded ice climbers on the Weeping Wall. A party of two climbers was stuck 60 meters above the ground. They had started climbing late in the morning, but when they had completed the route, another party was occupying the standard descent route in the Snivelling Gully. Therefore, the team decided to rappel via a rock descent route on the right hand side of the climb. The distance between anchors was greater than the length of their rope, and their descent was complicated by darkness. One climber rappelled to the end of the rope and was free-hanging. Eventually this climber managed to prusik back up the rope to his partner, at which point park wardens arrived to assist. The climbers did not have headlamps or other emergency equipment and were cold but uninjured. Flood lights were used to illuminate the waterfall.

Following instructions, the climbers lowered one end of their rope to park wardens, who were able to attach a rescue rope to it, thus providing enough rope for the climbers to descend to the base of the climb. The rescue was concluded by midnight.

Analysis

Inexperience is the primary cause of this incident. The climbers were very slow on the route, resulting in being caught by darkness. They were unfamiliar with the descent route they chose, not knowing that their rope would not reach. They did not carry headlamps, which would have been helpful. They did not consider the use of an Abalakov anchor, which would have allowed them to descend unaided. As ice climbing becomes increasingly popular, climbers become very technically proficient and capable, but often lack the experience to make sound judgments. (Source: Parks Canada Warden Service)

FAILURE TO FOLLOW ROUTE, OVERDUE
Alberta, Rocky Mountains, Mount Andromeda

Two climbers were two days overdue on the Skyladder route on Mount Andromeda.

On March 7, the climbers started climbing at 0300 and were at the base of Skyladder by dawn. They climbed the route in mixed weather with blowing snow. They summitted and walked to what they thought was the top of the AA Col descent route, arriving there at dusk. They dug in for the night and had a bivvy sac and down coats to keep them warm, but had no water. On March 8, they woke to poor visibility and strong SW winds. They started to descend the southeast ridge thinking it was the way to the AA Col. At 10,000 feet they left the ridge and began descending the upper glacier, working their way through crevasses and cliff bands. At dusk the second day, they were still attempting to find a route through the crevasses and cliffs, and bivouacked in a gully below some seracs. On March 9, day three at 1100, they began descending the gully to the glacier below, where they were spotted by the search and rescue helicopter. They were still 8 to 10 miles from the highway at this point.

Wardens flew over the area looking for the overdue party, and picked them up on the south side of Mount Andromeda when they were spotted. The climbers had absolutely no idea where they were on the mountain. They were convinced that they were on route and only a one-hour walk from their vehicle, whereas in fact, they were on the opposite side of the mountain descending difficult terrain to the Saskatchewan Glacier. Both climbers were uninjured, but were severely dehydrated from two days without water.

Analysis

Poor visibility and unfamiliarity with the descent route resulted in the climbers getting off route. Although they had a map and compass, they did not use them to find the AA Col descent route. The summit of Mount Andromeda is broad with several ridges leading off in different directions. It is common for climbers to get disoriented here, and end up descending the southeast ridge for a short ways in a white out. However, several clues should have made them question their location. Instead, they rationalized that somehow by continuing, they would eventually find the AA Col. When they were flown back to their vehicle, they were baffled at where they had ended up. (Source: Parks Canada Warden Service)

FALL ON ROCK, INADEQUATE PROTECTION, INEXPERIENCE
Alberta, Rocky Mountains, Mount Yamnuska

On May 13, D. B. reported a climbing accident to Bow Valley Provincial Park Rangers. The accident occurred on the second pitch of the Red Shirt Route on Mount Yamnuska. The leader, C. R., took a 40-foot fall and the fixed protection sling failed on impact, resulting in the leader falling past the first belay station. C. R. hit a ledge during the fall, resulting in an injured hip. C. R. credits his pack for taking much of the force of the fall, resulting in the injury being not as serious as it could have been. The Alberta Parks rescue team was heli-slung to the area and set up C. R. for a heli-sling evacuation.

Analysis

Unless one knows how long fixed slings have been in place, a backup is needed. Exposure to ultra-violet light causes nylon to deteriorate rapidly. (Source: George Field, Public Safety Specialist, Kananaskis Country)

FALL ON RAPPEL, INADEQUATE PROTECTION
Alberta, Rocky Mountains, Tunnel Mountain

On June 21, a party of two had completed the first two pitches of Gooseberry (II, 5.7) a seven-pitch popular route near the town of Banff. They had only planned to do those two pitches and then follow the walk-off ledge shown on the topo they had. The first climber started across the loose horizontal ledge using the rope with a rappel device as a safety. When she was about 20 meters across the ledge, she slipped and pendulumed across the face. The rope caught on the ledge about halfway between the rappel point and where she slipped.

She sustained facial lacerations, a cracked eye orbit and bruised shoulder and hip. A group of four including three certified ACMG guides were climbing nearby. They reported the accident to Warden Service Dispatch and lowered the injured climber to the base of the route. The climber was evacuated by heli-sling by a warden service rescue team to a waiting ambulance.

Analysis

Protecting traverses is important. In this case, it appears the party underestimated the consequences of a pendulum fall and were not familiar with other options for protecting a traverse. It was fortunate that the rope caught partway across the ledge. (Source: Parks Canada Warden Service)

AVALANCHE
Alberta, Rocky Mountains, Jasper National Park, Mount Edith Cavell

On June 28, two climbers ascended the East Ridge of Mount Edith Cavell, and made the summit by 1300. They began descending the East Ridge, and were over the steep section by 1500. At the head of the prominent gully which parallels the lower angled part of the ridge, they elected to remove the climbing rope and glissade the gully a short way. Recent snow and warm temperatures made conditions in the gully isothermal. A. M. was descending first and at 1510 triggered a small snow sluff which caused him to lose his footing. He started sliding down the gully and was unable to self-arrest. A. M. slid the entire length of the gully, approximately 1000 feet and came to rest just above the Col on a talus slope. His partner J. H. was also caught in the slough but managed to free himself before getting carried down. He scrambled down the ridge and found A. M.'s body at 1530. He did a primary survey and found that A. M. was deceased. J. H. then descended to the trailhead to report the occurrence to Park Wardens.

Analysis

The route was in poor condition with fresh, wet snow. Despite this, the climbers made extremely good time on the ascent and descent to the top of the gully. The gully is usually snow filled, which turns to hard firm in the spring and summer. Ten cm of wet spring snow, which fell recently, rested on a hard surface and sloughed easily. The gully probably looked like an inviting, easy and quick way to descend to avoid the tedium of descending greasy quartzite. Once the snow started moving, it would have been difficult to stop on the hard surface underneath. (Source: Parks Canada Warden Service)

FALL ON ROCK
Alberta, Rocky Mountains, Mount Yamnuska

On July 5, Kananaskis Emergency Services were notified by D. S. of a climbing accident on the Calgary Route of Mount Yamnuska. They responded by heli-slinging several rescuers to the base of the route. The rescuers climbed to the victim. J. H. was found conscious and stable with a possible broken hand, dislocated shoulder and other injuries. J. H. had taken a leader fall at approximately 1400, falling 30 feet after loosing his balance while trying to place gear.

J. H. was lowered from the fourth pitch to the second pitch from where he was slung out to a waiting ambulance. (Source: George Field, Public Safety Specialist, Kananaskis Country)

FALL ON ROCK, INADEQUATE BELAY-LOWERING
Alberta, Rocky Mountains, Heart Creek, Kananaskis Country
On July 18, M. P. was climbing at the Heart Creek sport climbing area when he was lowered off the end of his rope by his belayer, resulting in a six-meter fall. Injuries are unknown. He was evacuated by Peter Lougheed Park rangers. (Source: George Field, Public Safety Specialist, Kananaskis Country)

FALLING ROCK, OFF ROUTE, STRANDED
Alberta, Rocky Mountains, Mount Louis
On July 26, a party of two attempted Greenwood Route (III, 5.7) on the south Face of Mount Louis. They had difficulty following the route and found the climbing much more difficult than the 5.7 rating. Late in the day, one of the climbers was hit by a rock on the thigh. They were lost, discouraged and out of water on a south aspect during one of the hottest spells of weather recorded in the Rockies. They bivouacked with little gear (shorts and T-shirts), and at first light started yelling for help. At around 1330, a hiker passing below heard the calls and ran out to report them. A warden service rescue team responded and the pair were heli-slung off the steep face. They were dehydrated but otherwise OK.
Analysis
The party had mostly sport climbing experience. Route finding on some of the local longer limestone routes can be complex. In addition, the grades on routes put up in the sixties are sometimes considered "conservative" by modern climbers. (Source: Parks Canada Warden Service)

FALLING ROCK
Alberta, Rocky Mountains , Mount Fay
On August 2, a party of three were climbing the center ice bulge on the North Face Ice routes when one of the climbers was hit by rockfall, sustaining a lower leg fracture. The party lowered the injured climber to the glacier below. One of them then descended to Moraine Lake and reported the accident to Warden Service Dispatch. The injured climber was flown out by a warden service rescue team.
Analysis
The accident happened around 0830 during a very hot period of weather with little or no freezing at night. The 1998 summer in the Canadian Rockies was poor in general for routes subject to rockfall from melt. (Source: Parks Canada Warden Service)

STRANDED, OFF ROUTE, INEXPERIENCE
Alberta, Rocky Mountains, Mount Edith
On August 5, two climbers were attempting the South Ridge (II, 5.4) of Mount

Edith, but missed the start and got off route and onto steep limestone on the east face. They were lost and eventually both took leader falls trying to push a line towards the ridge. They gave up and then waited until they knew they would be overdue the next morning. A warden service rescue party flying back from another mission in the Lake Louise area flew by the mountain on the way back to Banff to check on the climbers. They knew the party was not due out till later, but were simply checking on their progress. The climbing party waved frantically to attract attention. In failing light and with an approaching lightning storm, a rescue party of two was placed on the ridge above by helicopter with a difficult toe-in landing. Bolts were drilled on the ridge and using a rope rescue winch. A rescuer was lowered down twice to raise the two climbers to the ridge. All four people bivouacked and were flown out at first light. Fortunately, all the lightning strikes during the night missed the ridge.

Analysis
This was the climbers' first route in the Rockies. They had rock climbed in Eastern Canada, but had no mountaineering experience. Missing the start of the route lead them into steep difficult limestone. (Source: Parks Canada Warden Service)

OVERDUE
Alberta, Rocky Mountains, Jasper National Park, Mount Geraldine
Two inexperienced climbers read the route description for Mount Geraldine in a local guidebook and decided that this was a reasonable objective for low-end climbers. Although Mount Geraldine is not technically difficult (mostly class 3), it is a very long one-day climb on steep and often loose quartzite, with a very difficult and steep descent. This was the fourth mountain the couple had ever climbed and the first in the Canadian Rockies. They departed the Geraldine Trail Head at 0900 on August 6, and took three hours to reach the base of the ridge (normally reached in an hour). They climbed the third class ridge (usually short roped, if a rope is used) in roped pitches, resulting in very slow progress. At 2200 they stopped to bivouac. They were out of water, but had lots of food. At 0600 on August 7, they started climbing again. They climbed through the day until 1930 when they made a second bivouac. At 0600 on August 8, they resumed climbing and reached the summit at 0900. The climbers were still on the summit at 1000 when rescuers made a fly-by.

Once rescuers located the overdue party by helicopter, they returned to the staging area to prepare for a heli-sling evacuation. By the time the rescuers were airborne again, the climbing party had gone part way down the descent gully from where they were evacuated by heli-sling.

Analysis
The climbers were very inexperienced. They were carrying heavy packs that included sleeping bags and foam pads, a fleece blanket, iodine, four quarts of water, and a map and compass. They had a full rock rack and full length 11mm rope. They assumed that it would be easier to go down the recommended descent route than to descend the ridge, and therefore kept climbing up instead of retreating when the ridge became intimidating. The route description

in the guidebook made the route sound easier than it is, and makes no mention of the difficulty of the descent. (Source: Parks Canada Warden Service)

FALLING ROCK
Alberta, Rocky Mountains, Mount Victoria

On August 12, a party of two were starting early up the North Ridge of Mount Victoria to the north peak after a bivouac at the Victoria Collier Col. The ridge is moderate ice with a fourth class rock step. At the step, the leader dislodged a rock which hit his belayer in the arm as he tried to protect his face. He sustained a fracture to the lower arm. Two other climbers leaving the bivouac below for the Collier ridge heard their call for help. One of them, an off-duty park warden, called Warden Service Dispatch on his radio. The injured climber was evacuated by heli-sling shortly afterwards. (Source: Parks Canada Warden Service)

FALL ON ROCK, PROTECTION PULLED, NO HARD HAT
Alberta, Rocky Mountains, Back-of-the-Lake Crag

On August 30, T. R. was leading "I Hear My Train A-Coming" (5.10c). He was retreating to his last piece because, "it was no good," when he fell, pulling it and at least one other piece. He hit the ground with the rope just coming tight possibly absorbing some of the shock. He lost consciousness and sustained head and neck injuries. He was not wearing a helmet. Two guides climbing nearby called Warden Service Dispatch and attended to the climbers injuries. The climber was flown out from the trail below the Crag.

Analysis

It is not known what gear the climber had placed. He obviously realized the importance of his last piece of protection, as he was attempting difficult moves and he was retreating to replace the piece. (Source: Parks Canada Warden Service)

FALL ON ROCK, PROTECTION PULLED OUT—PITON
Alberta, Rocky Mountains, Ha Ling Peak

On September 12, J. M., F. K. and S. K. were climbing the Northeast Ridge of Ha Ling Peak near Canmore. J. M. was leading the third last pitch when he experienced some difficulty and decided to be lowered and let someone else try the lead. He was lowered off a single existing piton which pulled out, sending him down a 30-foot fall. He suffered injuries to his shoulder and ankle. The group felt they could neither continue nor lower, so F. K. contacted Kananaskis Emergency Services for assistance.

KES responded by heli-slinging two rescuers to the site. The party was evacuated singly in screamer suits. At the heli staging area, the victim refused transportation to the Canmore Hospital.

(Editor's Note: Relying on a single piece of protection means it must be tested to determine whether it is "bomb proof." Trusting a "found" piton these days is a risk because of the length of time the piece may have been in place and an inability to test it.)

FALLING ROCK
Alberta, Rocky Mountains, Goat Mountain
On September 14 M.D.L.C. was climbing with D. C. on a route called Twilight Zone when he was hit in the right hand by rockfall. His thumb was badly crushed and almost amputated. D. C. called Kananaskis Emergency Services for assistance. K. E. S. responded with a helicopter and several EMS personnel. The EMS personnel were heli-slung to the base of the climb where D. C. had lowered the victim. M.D.L.C. was slung out in a screamer suit and then transported to the Banff Hospital for treatment. (Source: George Field, Public Safety Specialist, Kananaskis Country)

FALL ON ROCK, INADEQUATE BELAY—ROPE TOO SHORT
Alberta, Rocky Mountains, Back of the Lake Crag
On September 15, after completing Imaginary Grace (5.8), a climber was being lowered out from the anchors by his partner. The route is 30 meters long and their rope was 50 meters long. The rope went through the belay device and he fell 10 meters to the ground, sustaining ankle and back injuries. (Source: Parks Canada Warden Service)

AVALANCHE, FALL ON ICE, INADEQUATE PROTECTION
British Columbia, Rocky Mountains, Mount Dennis
On March 14, a party of three were climbing Guiness Gully (III, 4), a moderate ice route. The leader had completed the second pitch when a wet avalanche came down the gully. He had 50 meters of rope between him and the other two climbers at the belay below. The other two climbers had another 50 meters of rope stacked between them. None of the three climbers was clipped in to anchors. The upper climber managed to hug a tree at his belay and was not swept down. The two lower climbers were swept down with one of them ending up at the bottom of the first pitch, sustaining a forearm fracture and leg lacerations.

Warden service rescuers nearby witnessed the accident. Two rescuers ran up the approach to assess and treat the injured climber. The injured climber was heli-slung to a waiting ambulance shortly afterwards. The other two climbers, as well as other climbers on nearby routes, were evacuated by heli-sling, as well as other climbers on nearby routes due to the extreme avalanche hazard.
Analysis
As with many waterfall ice routes in the Rockies, avalanche hazard is a constant concern. When climbers left the parking area that morning, it was raining lightly. Unfortunately most of them did not see that as an indication of rapidly increasing avalanche hazard. (Source: Parks Canada Warden Service)

FALL ON ROCK, CLIMBING UNROPED
British Columbia, Selkirk Mountains, Grays Peak
Two climbers departed the Gibson Lake parking lot in the early morning of July 16 and traveled through dense bush for several hours to the base of the west face

of Grays Peak. Their objective was to traverse Grays Peak via the Southwest Ridge.

The weather was clear, with the temperature at 14 degrees C, and a light wind blowing from the southwest. During the night, extensive dew had formed, so both the brush and the granite slabs were wet.

Upon reaching the base of the face, the climbers put their helmets on and began scrambling through fourth class terrain on the west face towards the ridge crest. The climbers were moving beside one another to minimize rock fall exposure. They arrived at a sloping, grassy bench 20 meters deep that bisected the face. One moved into what appeared to be a steeper section of terrain, while the other continued upwards. "A few minutes later I called down to J. and he said he was going to traverse over to where I had ascended." She continued 80 meters higher and waited just below the ridge crest. Ten minutes passed. She heard the distinct sound of a falling object, but no call.

The time was 1105. She scrambled 50 meters back down to the bench on the west face where she expected to find her fallen partner. Upon reaching the bench, there was no sign of him and she received no reply to any calls. She searched the area extensively and then from the edge, saw him 70 meters below on the steep face. He was not moving, lying on his chest on a small ledge with his legs tangled among some small sub-alpine firs.

Since her partner had the rope in his pack, it took some time for her to reach him. Assessing his injuries, she determined that he had a fractured neck, fractured lumbar spine, fractured right femur and extensive lacerations. His level of consciousness (LOC) was low.

She removed his pack, repositioned him, supported his head and neck and covered him. It was 1210, and they were at an elevation of 2000 meters. She assessed the site for rescue potential and then proceeded to descend 650 meters to the Gibson Lake access road for assistance.

She reached the road at 1250 and was picked up by a local doctor and driven 14 km to the West Kootenay Parks office. National Parks was contacted and dispatched from Canmore with long-lining equipment. A local helicopter was deployed from Nelson with medical equipment and a mountain guide. The helicopter picked her and the doctor up and they returned to the accident site at 1545.

The rescue team flew over the west face and could see clothing and equipment, but no sign of the injured climber. On the third pass, he was seen 20 meters below on the edge of the steep cliff face. The team was dropped on the bench above and descended to him. He was in an inverted position with his helmet and most of his clothing removed. He had sustained head injuries.

The team rigged a series of fixed lines on the cliff edge and secured him. National Parks arrived on the scene, and the victim was long-lined down to Gibson Lake and then transferred into the first helicopter and flown to Nelson. A trauma team flew from Vancouver and transported the victim to Vancouver General Hospital.

Analysis

The injured climber remembers no details of the fall. Since he did not call out, both climbers assume he either slipped on the damp granite or a foothold broke loose and he was knocked out immediately. He survived an initial fall of 80 meters and then a series of second falls. His back fracture/dislocation (at T-12 and L-1) indicates a fall directly onto his back with his legs folding forward.

He was wearing a full pack with both his chest and waist strap buckled up. This pack absorbed a significant portion of the impact. His helmet was very well secured after the initial fall. This accident is an excellent example of how even though the climbing may not be that technical for competent climbers, the consequences of a fall in this terrain can be extremely serious.

The weather and time of day contributed to the positive outcome of this rescue. Long-lining equipment is not available locally and was a critical component of the extrication from the cliff face. It is doubtful if the victim would have survived overnight if sling rescue had been unavailable. He received surgery to realign the spine. After rehabilitation, he has made a full recovery.

The route was not in ideal conditions. Even though they were in fourth class terrain, a rope would have been a good idea. (Source: Parks Canada Warden Service)

FALL ON RAPPEL
British Columbia, Rocky Mountains, Mount Stanley
On July 27, after returning from the North Face glacier route, three climbers were rappelling low angle slabs heading to the meadows below. One of them lost control of his rappel for a short distance and caught his foot in a crack. He fractured his ankle. His two partners then assisted him down to their camp below. When they became overdue the next morning, a warden service rescue team was dispatched. The injured climber was flown to the hospital.
Analysis
It is not known if the climber had a prusik backup to his rappel. (Source: Parks Canada Warden Service)

OFF ROUTE, PARTY SEPARATED, INEXPERIENCE
British Columbia, Selkirk Mountains, Avalanche Peak
Two climbers on Avalanche Peak found themselves separated. One of the climbers with no previous experience down-climbed a series of small cliffs until he found himself looking down a 200-meter vertical drop. Unable to climb back up the cliff bands he had jumped down, he settled in to wait. His partner, who described himself as very experienced, reached the bottom and spotted the stranded climber. Two hikers were sent for help.

An HRS equipped helicopter was working in the area. The stranded climber was slung out by the Warden Service to Rogers Pass.
Analysis
This situation saw an experienced climber leaving an inexperienced climber to find his own way down, resulting in the climber becoming stranded. (Source: Parks Canada Warden Service)

UNITED STATES

FALL ON SNOW, UNABLE TO SELF-ARREST, FALL INTO CREVASSE, INADEQUATE PROTECTION, WEATHER
Alaska, Mount McKinley, West Buttress

On May 26 at 1431, Australian climber John Sides (29), a member of the AUSPAT expedition, fell while descending the Rescue Gully on Denali. Sides slid 300 feet to the brink of a crevasse, then fell down into it and came to rest on a snow bridge.

The AUSPAT expedition had spent three days at High Camp (17,200 feet) waiting out bad weather to make a summit attempt on Denali. On May 26 AUSPAT made an attempt for the summit, but turned back before Denali Pass because the wind speed had increased. The three climbers decided to abandon their climb and descend to 14,200 feet. Although the weather had improved compared to the preceding three days, the higher wind speed now became a factor in their decision making. AUSPAT elected to descend the Rescue Gully because there was a fixed line in there, and the gully was thought to be less exposed than the normal route up on the ridge.

Around noon, AUSPAT began descending the old fixed line in the gully. The line was short, and from its end the climbers decided to continue down unroped to each other. At first, the cramponing was reliable and easy, but midway down, sections where fresh snow had accumulated were slippery.

At 1430, the climbers stopped for a brief rest. Sides' feet slipped out from beneath him and when he attempted to sit down, he started sliding. Sides attempted to self-arrest and almost succeeded, but he hit some rougher patches of snow, which sent him sliding 300 feet to the brink of a crevasse. Sides then disappeared into the crevasse.

Brandon and Ferris made their way down to the crevasse and looked down into it from the lower lip. They could not see Sides or get a response when they called out his name. (Sides was unconscious and unable to respond.) Brandon and Ferris used their CB radio to call the Ranger Camp to ask for assistance, but did not get a reply. At 1530 Brandon and Ferris heard Sides call out for help from 135 feet down, deep within the crevasse. Ferris rappelled down into the crevasse and sighted Sides. It appeared to Ferris that Sides had free fallen a short span, but—fortunately—slid most of the total distance down a snow ramp and ended up resting on a snow bridge.

NPS personnel and volunteers had witnessed the accident from 14,200 feet and alerted the Incident Command System. Volunteers organized a hasty rescue team and started up to the accident site to assist in crevasse extrication, transport and patient care.

Ferris performed a patient assessment of Sides and assisted him part way up the snow ramp. At 1746 volunteers arrived on the scene and rigged a hauling system to extricate Sides the remainder of the way out of the crevasse. On the surface, Sides was reassessed and stabilized.

The remaining AUSPAT members, Scott Ferris and Scott Brandon, along with NPS volunteers, rescued Sides and transported him to the medical tent at 14,200 feet, where he was treated for a pneumothorax and hypothermia. At 2253 Sides was evacuated by the LAMA helicopter to base camp, where he was then transported by a Pavehawk helicopter and flown directly to Alaska Regional Hospital in Anchorage.

Analysis

Recently there have been several accidents related to climbers sitting down to rest and falling during the process. One was fatal. In these incidents neither climber was roped or anchored. Perhaps Sides' fall could have been prevented if he had tied into his ice ax and had set it as an anchor before he rested. (Source: Kevin Moore, Mountaineering Ranger)

FALL ON ICE/SNOW, UNABLE TO SELF-ARREST, WEATHER
Alaska, Mount McKinley, West Buttress

(What follows is a synopsis of two incidents, one that happened as a result of the second party attempting to rescue the first.)

At 1130 on May 24, Jason Sinnes and Daniel Rowarth (29)—Burrito Brothers climbing team—decided to descend from the 17,000 foot campsite on the West Buttress route of Mount McKinley, where they had spent the previous night. They felt that weather conditions (which had been generally poor for the duration of their trip) were once again deteriorating. Mike Vanderbeek (33) and Tim Hurtado, National Park Service volunteer patrol members, had been at 17K for three days and had spent the two previous nights there. The NPS team was feeling well with "only slight headaches the night before." They had originally planned to attempt the North Summit of the peak. Since the weather was getting worse again, they had delayed their departure for the NPS camp at 14,000 feet in hopes of being able to assist with the delivery of a helicopter sling load to 17K. After learning that the helicopter mission had been canceled, Vanderbeek and Hurtado began their descent at 1300. The climbers both had "full summit gear" on and carried 30–40 pound packs. Each wore climbing harnesses, crampons, and overboots. They were each carrying one snow picket and one ice screw. They were not carrying bivouac gear, since they had used the patrol equipment available in the NPS cache at 17K. Winds at that time were steady at 30 mph with gusts to 60–70 mph. They discussed the need to be very careful with foot placement since "a misstep could be fatal."

Moving steadily, Vanderbeek and Hurtado overtook the Canadian pair some time during the next hour around 16,900 feet. Sinnes and Rowarth considered themselves fortunate to be in "close proximity to the rangers" and were glad that "every few hundred feet the rangers would wait for us." At a point just above Washburn's Thumb, the large, well-known granite monolith along this section of the route, Vanderbeek's crampon came off his boot. (Over his climbing boots he had been wearing Forty Below neoprene overboots and Lowe Footfang crampons.) Sinnes and Rowarth caught up to them again at this point.

After getting his crampon back on, Vanderbeek, accompanied by Hurtado, climbed down below the Thumb, followed shortly thereafter by Sinnes. After down-climbing the steep, fixed section near the Thumb, Rowarth rejoined Sinnes and they regrouped at a flat area of the ridge. According to Sinnes, Rowarth said that "he felt fine, not tired or anything." They continued down the ridge, staying slightly to the lee side. Sinnes described it as "slightly off the beaten track, steep, and slightly technical." Sinnes stated that this section "caught him [Rowarth] by surprise and he lost purchase with his feet." The approximate time of Rowarth's fall from the ridge was 1400.

Vanderbeek and Hurtado were about 100 feet away from Rowarth when he fell. Hurtado had turned around to "see how Jason and Daniel were doing" and saw Rowarth 50 feet below the ridge crest, catapulting downward. They could not see very far down from their vantage point so Vanderbeek traversed over to the fall line and found Rowarth's ice ax. Hurtado retrieved the radio from Vanderbeek's pack, but could not get out from that location. Vanderbeek therefore hiked over the ridge to the south so that he could transmit. Ten to twenty minutes later Vanderbeek returned to Hurtado and Sinnes' position. Hurtado's understanding of the situation and the plan at that point was:

- Vanderbeek and Hurtado had been given permission from Mountaineering Park Ranger Daryl Miller at 14K to establish contact with Rowarth.
- Adrian Nature was going to be dispatched from 14K to 16K to provide a necessary communications link at 16K since they would presumably be out of radio contact once they started down off the south side of the ridge crest.
- Upon further contact from Vanderbeek and Hurtado, additional resources would be available from 14K.

Hurtado stated that visibility was 200 feet, winds were 30–35 mph gusting to 40–45 mph and higher. It was not very cold and it did not appear to be unreasonable to be traveling in these weather conditions. At this point they met two climbers, Rowan Laver and Gordon Cox, ascending the ridge to put in a cache at 17K. Cox agreed to assist Sinnes back down to 16K. Hurtado and Vanderbeek consolidated gear for the descent down toward the Peters Glacier. According to Laver, Vanderbeek could "see something down on the glacier." Vanderbeek and Hurtado took a shovel, tent fly and poles from Sinnes and added this to their other light bivouac equipment. Hurtado and Vanderbeek stopped briefly and had a discussion of how best to proceed with the descent. They talked about using a rope, but felt that rope work would be slower and that they thought they could perform a self-arrest under the present conditions. Hurtado recalled that Vanderbeek seemed more concerned with what he [Hurtado] thought, as he was the less experienced climber. They began to descend the ridge at 1430, winding their way down from Rowarth's ice ax which they left in place.

Hurtado reported that the terrain that he and Vanderbeek encountered during their descent consisted of "600–800 feet of hard snow" with occasional patches of ice "not more than 10–30 feet long." They were in voice contact with one another descending 10–15 feet apart, and left and right of the fall line which was marked by occasional patches of blood. Hurtado stated that he and Vanderbeek "maintained continual voice contact, determining each other's fatigue and comfort level" and that Mike had relayed pointers regarding different descending techniques. Hurtado's goggles became fogged and his visibility became limited to about three feet up or down. In Hurtado's words, "I was mostly feeling my way down the terrain." They now encountered an extensive ice patch and Hurtado, facing in, became much more deliberate with his tool placements. (Each carried a single, 70 cm ice ax.) He described the ice as being in the 40–50 degree range and as being "very brittle and the first swing often dinner-plated." While descending, Hurtado was not aware that the ice patch was extensive, but rather assumed that it was another occasional patch of ice which would be followed by snow, which had been the pattern to this point. They descended this particular ice patch for 10–15 minutes when Hurtado requested that they head for some rocks that they could see in order to stop and reevaluate. Vanderbeek replied, "Okay." Hurtado stated that, at that time, he felt "it might be wise to rope and use a running belay." They continued down toward the rocks and once again made voice contact. Two or three minutes later, at 1345, Hurtado heard "the sound of nylon on ice." He heard nothing else and shouted for Vanderbeek and received no answer. He removed his goggles, could see much better and realized that his position was precarious. He was on a "400–500 foot sheet of hard, blue water ice that was 45–55 degrees." As he continued to descend toward the rocks for 10–15 feet, the full gravity of the situation hit him. Hurtado decided that the best course of action was to place his one ice screw and anchor himself to that. This accomplished, he ate, drank and began to chop a ledge on the ice sheet for himself. Hurtado realized that Nature was on his way and that he could wait for a rescue.

At 1426 Adrian Nature left the 14K NPS camp carrying little more than a radio and personal gear (excluding sleeping bag and bivouac equipment). He reached 16K one hour and fifty-six minutes. There he met up with Rowan Laver. They roped up and proceeded up the ridge to where Rowarth had disappeared. Nature spoke of being in "rescue mode" as opposed to "climber mode." He differentiated between the two by stating that when in "rescue mode," he was roped up with a partner, and they safeguarded their travel through the use of running belays or fixed anchored belays, depending upon terrain and conditions. Nature's plan was to check in with 14K at 15-minute intervals. Gordon Cox was enlisted as Nature's replacement to serve as the vital communication link between 14K and the second rescue team (Nature and Laver).

At 1646 a support party consisting of four additional volunteer patrol members left the 14K NPS camp bound for 16K. The group consisted of Dr. Mark Elstad, Linda Davis, Dean Giampietro (volunteers on Daryl Miller's patrol), and Dr. Colin Grissom (volunteer on Billy Shott's patrol with extensive Denali experience, as well as a great deal of other high altitude climbing experience from around the world.)

After they reached the accident site, Nature and Laver attempted to contact Vanderbeek and Hurtado by radio but were unsuccessful. They descended one pitch through the rocks, and screamed for Vanderbeek and Hurtado between wind gusts (60–70 mph). During one relatively calm period they heard someone scream, "Help!" They contacted Miller at 14K at 1730, relayed that they had voice contact, and requested permission to begin down-climbing. Permission was granted to try and contact Vanderbeek and Hurtado. They down-climbed one pitch and requested permission to continue, which was granted. They continued their belayed descent into gradually steepening and progressively more technical terrain. According to Laver it was five full rope lengths down to Hurtado's position (750–800 feet). They encountered hard, blue ice for the final 200–300 feet. At 1751 Jay Hudson left Talkeetna Airport for the McKinley area to provide an additional radio relay link during the operation and at 1829 an Air Force C130 aircraft was requested by the Incident Command Post (ICP) located at the Talkeetna Ranger Station. At 1914 the Nature/Laver rescue team reached Hurtado's location and they continued down roped together as a party of three. As they descended through the rock band, they found Vanderbeek's sun glasses and ice ax. As they neared the bottom, they noticed a blood trail that was one foot wide and that led directly to the body of Daniel Rowarth, located one rope length from the bergschrund on the flat floor of the glacier. Vanderbeek's pack was found approximately 50 feet up-glacier of Rowarth's body, while Rowarth's pack was found about 150 feet down-glacier. Both packs were strap-side down, and the waist, shoulder, and chest buckles and straps were intact and not broken.

Communications with the ground team were pretty good at this point as both Jay Hudson and the Air Force C130 were circling in the area. An attempt to utilize the NPS exclusive-use contract helicopter (SA315 B LAMA) to assist with an aerial search proved fruitless when mountaineering ranger Kevin Moore and pilot Jim Hood decided to turn back from the SE Fork of the Kahiltna in whiteout conditions. Adrian Nature described the weather conditions in terms of some of the worst Alaskan/Denali storms he had experienced. On a 1–10 scale with 10 being the worst, he described the overall condition as an "8."

After Nature's team's official search efforts were fruitless, their main focus shifted to that of self-preservation. They managed to retrieve a tent and a sleeping bag from Rowarth's pack. Their instructions from Colin Grissom, leader of the support team at 16K, had been to "come out of the hole." They attempted to do so, but in the swirling winds and whiteout, they found that they had traversed too far to the west down the glacier.

At the 14K camp Daryl Miller had enlisted the help of Dave Langrish and John Elwell (Firestarters Expedition) and at 1836 had led the trio carrying a 600 foot rope and overnight gear to the base of the fixed lines and back to the 14K camp. The group returned at midnight, traveling in "hideous" weather after having hooked up with Gordon Cox and Jason Sinnes on their descent to 14K. Miller had also contacted Ryan Hokanson and Kirby Spangler, a pair of strong climbers who had originally been at the 14K camp to attempt the Cassin

Ridge. Hokanson and Spangler had returned exhausted at 1600 from an aborted attempt on the upper West Rib and declined Miller's original request for assistance, saying that they needed rest and rehydration. They did offer to assist the following day.

(Editor's Note: Over the next four days, search efforts continued. Twenty NPS personnel, eleven volunteers, and seven emergency hires participated. Extreme weather marked the first two of these days, then it cleared. Rowarth's body and the two packs were recovered, but, though many small items belonging to Vanderbeek were found, including his face mask, there were no signs of his body. The search was called off on May 29.

An investigation team was assembled, and the part of their analysis pertaining to the cause of Vanderbeek's fall and some of the subsequent actions follows below.)

Analysis

The accident was an unwitnessed slip on a 45 degree ice slope. Whether a crampon came off, the wind blew Vanderbeek off the ice, or he slipped from his ice ax or crampons is unknown. The decision to descend the slope unroped in high winds with limited visibility was the major contributing factor. Descending unroped and unprotected by a rope and anchors produced a situation where there was no way to arrest the fall, given the terrain encountered. Mike Vanderbeek was never located and is presumed to have come to rest in either the bergschrund or a crevasse on the Peters Glacier.

The following factors were analyzed for their contribution to the accident:

Communications and Decisions. The decision to descend and look for Rowarth was the first critical decision in the incident. Immediately after Rowarth's fall, Vanderbeek radioed Daryl Miller at the 14,000 foot camp to report the accident. After a short discussion, Vanderbeek told Miller he could not see the bottom, but if he could "take a look" a short distance lower he could probably spot him. Miller discussed with Vanderbeek the importance of maintaining communications and that Adrian Nature would head up with a radio to act as a human repeater on the ridge. Miller felt that Vanderbeek and Hurtado would take a short look and try to determine what had happened to Rowarth, but would wait for Nature to maintain good communications.

After speaking with Miller, Vanderbeek descended off the ridge to where Hurtado and Sinnes were waiting. It was Hurtado's understanding that they had permission to descend and begin a search for Rowarth.

The physical communications network between the Talkeetna Ranger Station, the 7,000 foot camp and the 14,000 foot camp consists of hand-held FM radios and cell phones. Generally, communication between the three areas is good. Communications are more difficult in remote spots on the mountain. The park currently has sufficient radios to outfit each team of rangers or volunteers. However, there are not enough to supply each one on the mountain. In addition, CB radios are used by the Base Camp Manager and climbers. The ranger patrols monitor the CB broadcasts.

Communications between the Vanderbeek/Hurtado team and the 14,000 foot camp disappeared as the team descended the side of the ridge toward the

Peters Glacier. Only Vanderbeek had a park radio, which was strapped to his chest. After he fell, Hurtado was unable to communicate with Nature, who was making his way up the ridge. Only by screaming was Hurtado able to make his position known to Nature when he reached the accident site.

Witnessed Fall. Many of those interviewed surmised that the impact of witnessing Daniel Rowarth's fall created a great sense of urgency to aid the victim. This "rescue fever" is not uncommon in life and death situations, whether among firefighters in burning buildings, or on mountain sides. The heightened sense of urgency produces a desire for speed and a sacrifice of personal safety. The objective facts to not indicate any sense of panic or any initial poor judgment or rash decisions. On the contrary, the opposite was indicated, and Vanderbeek and Hurtado discussed their decisions and proceeded accordingly. Nevertheless, the impact of a witnessed fall cannot be ignored.

Several of those interviewed used the term "rescue mode" when speaking of both the procedures and mind-set they were operating under during the search. This meant, among other things, that they would use all necessary precautions, rope up, set adequate anchors, maintain constant communications, and follow a line of authority in decision making.

The Rope. The decision not to use the climbing rope was the second critical decision in the incident. Vanderbeek and Hurtado had a rope available, stowed in Vanderbeek's pack. They made a mutual decision not to use the rope. The ground where they started the search was fairly easy, and it looked from their vantage that they could descend safely without it. As the ground steepened, they continued to discuss roping up, asking each other if they still felt comfortable on the steeper terrain. When the snow changed to ice, Hurtado finally asked Vanderbeek to move toward the rocks so that they could rope up.

Weather. The wind was blowing steadily at an estimated 30–40 mph; gusts well above 40 mph were described by witnesses. The temperature was well below freezing. Visibility was variable due to the blowing snow and clouds. At times the Peters Glacier was visible 2,000 feet below, and at other times the climbers could see only a few feet ahead. Hurtado describes how, even wearing goggles, he had extremely limited visibility, and after the goggles began to ice up, he could see only three feet and often felt his way down.

Terrain. The route from 16,000 feet to 17,000 feet on Mount McKinley for the most part follows the ridge line, winding on snow between granite rocks. The routes stays to the north side of the ridge. The slope toward the Peters Glacier is 45–50 degrees and about 2,000 feet high. Depending on the wind and snow cover, ice and rock appear discontinuously along the slope. Most private parties do not use a rope along this section. Guided parties rope their clients up. A section next to "Washburn's Thumb" has fixed ropes into which most parties clip a carabiner or ascending device for protection. The altitude at Washburn's Thumb where the initial accident occurred is approximately 16,500 feet.

Equipment. Both Vanderbeek and Hurtado carried one ice screw and one snow picket each, a standard number for the West Buttress route. This would not have been enough protection for a safe descent using the rope 2,000 feet down a steep slope. The leader would have to have placed several pickets or ice screws on a 150 foot lead down the snow slope to have safely anchored the belayer and protected the second person climbing down—just the opposite technique of leading up a similar slope. The lack of protection may have been a factor in the decision not to use the rope; a fall of one of the two would have been fatal to both without a sufficient number or pickets or ice screws.

Each carried one standard 70 cm ice ax. It is not possible to self-belay with one ice ax as it would be with two ice tools, where one tool would always be attached to the ice while placing the other. In using one tool, whenever it is extracted from the ice, the climber is without protection. During the interview, Ryan Hokanson stated that he was "very surprised that Mike had downclimbed the ice with one ax—shocked."

Each wore crampons. One of Hurtado's crampons slipped off his boot at the start of the descent, just out of camp. He explained that their overboots made it difficult to have the bail of the crampons grab the boot welt securely. Vanderbeek's crampon slipped off just before Washburn's Thumb, and he re-attached it. This may have been an immediate cause of his slip on the ice. One crampon was found among the rocks on the fall line. The crampons have two front points, one of which was broken. It was analyzed by a metallurgist at Black Diamond Equipment, who determined that the break occurred as a result of a high impact, most likely during the fall, thus ruling it out as a cause of the fall.

Beyond the first short distance on the moderate angle snow slope, the team did not have adequate equipment to protect their descent.

Experience. Mike Vanderbeek was a very experienced mountaineer with a long resume of difficult climbs on various high altitude peaks, including Mount McKinley. Vanderbeek had significantly more experience than Hurtado, particularly in the Alaska Range; however, Hurtado had climbed on McKinley previously. Hurtado, a third-year medical student, had participated in SAR incidents with the El Paso search and rescue team. Vanderbeek did not list any SAR experience or training in his resume. Their level of experience and expertise would not lead one to expect to find them in a compromising situation. (Source: Daryl Miller, Mountaineering Ranger, and Investigating Team, consisting of Ralph Tingey, Reynold Jackson, Jay Liggett, and Jay Cabler.)

FALL ON SNOW, UNABLE TO SELF-ARREST, DESCENDING UNROPED, WEATHER
Alaska, Mount McKinley, West Buttress

The Rainier Mountaineering, Inc. guided trip led by chief guide Phil Ershler and assistant guide Chris Hooyman began their expedition on May 21. The group, consisting of four clients and two guides, took nine days to reach the 14,200 foot camp. During this time, one of the clients was escorted to base camp and flown back to Talkeetna due to a minor foot injury. The group spent the next five nights at 14,200 feet while incorporating a carry to 17,200 feet.

On June 3 the party established camp at 17,200 feet on the West Buttress. On June 4 the party of five reached the summit in good weather, descended to their camp at 17,200 feet, and spent the night hoping to descend further the next day. On June 5 the group awoke to poor weather and decided to stay until visibility increased and winds decreased. Later that day, around 1600, the group broke camp hoping to take advantage of a weather window to descend to 14,200 feet. Before the group could descend to the 17,000 foot level on the West Buttress ridge, high winds were encountered and chief guide Ershler decided to return to 17,200 feet, set up camp, and again wait for better weather to descend. The National Weather Service forecast broadcast that evening was for a "wind event" storm to begin the evening of June 6.

On June 6, Ershler left camp mid-morning and visually checked the weather from atop the West Buttress ridge. The weather had improved and the RMI group broke camp and began to descend along with at least two other groups. The group of five began descending as a single team, using one rope of four climbers and adding a second rope linked to the fourth climber. The last and fifth climber (Hooyman) was tied in ten meters behind the fourth, with the remainder of the rope coiled and carried in the compression straps of his pack. The rope team was as follows: first on the rope was chief guide Phil Ershler, second was client Larry Semento, third was client Mike Van Stratten, fourth was client Meegan Pyle, and fifth (linked with separate rope to Pyle) was guide Chris Hooyman. The party chose to descend as a single rope team (incorporating a second rope) to better utilize running belays, specifically the many rocks on the snow ridge as natural protection.

Between 1100 and 1130 the team had descended in moderate winds, with gusts and visibility of about 160 feet, to a point on the West Buttress ridge at 17,100 feet. At this point the route traverses parallel to and just north of the ridge top. While traversing, Semento slipped and fell a short distance on the slope. Ershler utilized a rock as protection between himself and Semento, took out all slack in the system, and held Semento on tension to prevent him from slipping any further down the slope. Semento was unable to get up. Witnesses described a feeling or urgency in the situation due to the location and weather. As Ershler was yelling instructions to Semento, Pyle reports that Hooyman approached her, unclipped his rope from her harness, and began descending toward Semento, probably to assist. Pyle also reports that she initially told Hooyman to stay tied in to her, and then yelled ahead to have Hooyman clip into Van Stratton. While descending, Hooyman fell on the 35 to 40 degree snow slope. Witnesses report that he dropped his ice ax and was unable to self-arrest. They watched him accelerate onto the steeper slope below and begin to tumble end over end toward the Peters Glacier.

Without contact and unable to see Hooyman, Ershler, with the help of a private party and another RMI group, took his team back to 17,200 feet and established camp. In deteriorating weather, Ershler fixed approximately 500 feet of rope down Hooyman's fall line (using Hooyman's ice ax as a reference), but was unable to find any sign of Hooyman. At 1417, while Ershler was descending the fixed lines, climbers at the 17,200 foot camp reported the accident to NPS Rangers at the 14,200 foot camp. Ershler ascended to the accident site and joined RMI guide Jeff Ward, who had acquired lines again and searched approximately 700 feet below the fall point. Again, no signs of Hooyman were found. Increasing winds and poor visibility forced Ershler and Ward back to the group's camp at 17,200 feet. That evening the forecasted storm hit the mountain and no one was able to travel anywhere above the 11,000 foot level for the next 36 hours.

When the weather improved on June 8, Ershler and his group were able to descend while four NPS personnel ascended to the accident site from 14,200 feet. Nine hundred feet of rope were fixed down the fall line and two NPS personnel searched the area for several hours. Nothing was found in the search. No other ground searches were conducted. On June 13, the weather permitted an air search with the NPS helicopter, which found and recovered Hooyman's body with the use of a remote grabber. Hooyman's body had taken a fall line that brought him below and to the west of the fall site, where he stopped at 16,000 feet.

Analysis

Experience. Chris Hooyman's mountaineering experience includes several Northwest area ascents on both technical and glaciated peaks. This expedition was Hooyman's first on Denali. RMI's apprenticeship system is in place, whereby senior guides help evaluate assistant guides. Hooyman's evaluations, both written and verbal, were good with several senior guides praising his technical and people skills. Phil Ershler stated that Hooyman was comfortable on all terrain found on the West Buttress of Denali.

RMI's Standard Operating Procedures. RMI's documentation states that, "All guides and clients should be roped at all times on the McKinley routes, except within an established camp area, emergency situations…" As Larry Semento's fall on the ridge does not qualify as an emergency, and as there were other options available to render assistance, Hooyman disregarded RMI's safety policy when he unclipped from the rope team.

Unclipping from the Rope Team. When Chris Hooyman unclipped from Meegan Pyle, he put himself at a greater risk of taking a serious fall and decreased the safety margin of the rope team. Chris Hooyman acted independently when he unclipped his rope from the team. He did not communicate his intentions to any person and was told by at least one client to reclip into the rope team before descending to Larry Semento. Although traveling unroped is a common practice for skilled climbers in this type of terrain, this is not the first accident where an experienced climber/guide was injured or killed because he chose to unrope or put slack in a rope team in order to handle a situation more rapidly.

Weather. The weather, specifically the wind, did not allow for discussion between the two guides. If it were possible, dialogue between Hooyman and chief guide Phil Ershler may have prevented the accident. The wind may also be directly responsible for the fall itself. Two out of the five witnesses interviewed believe that Hooyman was literally pushed over by the wind. The other witnesses believe it was a combination of the wind and Hooyman's footing. The sense of urgency described by those who were interviewed was also amplified by the weather. In calmer conditions Hooyman may not have felt the need to unrope and help his client. Ershler had decided to postpone descending on the morning of June 5 due to poor weather, and later that same day decided to return to the 17,200 foot camp after beginning to descend and experiencing high wind. The weather on the ridge the morning of June 6 was less than perfect, but substantially better than the previous day. The forecasted "wind event" which was to begin in the evening of June 6 may have contributed to deciding to descend that morning, but it is apparent that the group was prepared to wait if they needed to. The group, specifically Ershler, was aware of the increased risks and difficulties the weather could potentially impose when descending the ridge from 17,200 feet. (Source: From a Denali National Park and Preserve Case Incident Record)

FALL INTO MOAT—SNOW BRIDGE COLLAPSED, POOR POSITION
Alaska, Chugach Range, Cantata Peak

On June 6, around 1400, Kirk Towner (26) and I (29) were in the process of descending from Cantata Peak (5,205 feet). After glissading almost 2,000 feet down a prominent snow gully on the southwest face, we traversed the snow slope on the north side of the ice-covered glacial tarn that is the headwaters of a small creek that flows into a lower valley before emptying into Symphony Lake. Due to heavy, late-winter snow storms the area was still covered in four to six feet of packed, granular ("spring") snow which was relatively easy to travel on, but that obscured many terrain features.

At the outlet of the lake, the slope levels off, so we removed our crampons knowing that ahead there was only one relatively easy glissade of approximately 500 feet that would take us to the valley floor. We continued walking along the north side of the creek which disappeared under the snowpack shortly after leaving the lake. Just before the slope began to angle downward toward the lower valley, I suddenly broke through a snow bridge that spanned the glacial creek. I was instantly swept downstream and over a 40-foot waterfall that was completely hidden under a winter's-worth of snow where the creek drops into a narrow gorge as it descends toward the valley floor.

I landed on my back in a pool of freezing water where the snow pinched down toward the rock. I was able to pull myself up to stand on a narrow ledge after nearly drowning. Luckily, I was still conscious and realized that my predicament was serious. I had to remove my backpack because it was so heavy. I didn't think I could move out of the main flow of the waterfall without falling. Leaning against the snow wall, I unbuckled the waist belt and let the pack drop behind me. It disappeared into the rushing water beneath my feet. I then carefully moved to the right out of the main flow on my little ledge. I saw a small hole about 40 feet above me where light was coming in. I attempted to climb out of the cave by stemming between the slippery rock (under the waterfall) and the snow wall (approximately a yard apart) while using my ice ax to pull up on. I made it up about eight feet, before my foot slipped off the snow and I fell back into the narrow gap where I started.

My partner did not see me fall, as he was approximately 150 feet ahead of me below a bulge in the snow slope. The accident had happened so quickly that my screams were instantly muffled. After five minutes of waiting, he climbed back up the slope and realized what had happened. Fortunately, he eventually saw the same small hole near the top of the waterfall and, after hearing my yells for help, was able to lower his ice ax on a 35-foot makeshift sling of pieced-together anchor webbing. (I had been carrying the rope, which was in my pack.) I wrapped the sling of the second ax around my wrist several times before grasping it, then pulled myself up the waterfall in several exhausting moves, using my ice ax and Kirk's sling (which he pulled on from above).

By the time I got out of the hole, I had been in the near freezing water for almost 35 minutes. I was very hypothermic and my hands were completely numb. Luckily, I had sustained relatively minor injuries—a couple of gashes on my left knee and a blow to the face that had knocked out several teeth in my upper jaw. It was raining fairly hard, so the best course of action was to get moving so that I could warm myself up and keep from getting stiff.

After I was out of the hole, Kirk put all the clothes he could spare on me. We then traversed about 150 feet to the right and glissaded down the final slope into the valley, with me sitting behind Kirk as he braked with his ax. It took us three hours to hobble back to our camp two miles down the valley, where Kirk got me into dry clothes and the sleeping bags. Within a few minutes of lying down, my back and legs became so stiff that I couldn't sit up or even roll over. After brewing up hot drinks for me and getting some food for himself, Kirk headed down the five-mile trail to call for a rescue, since we did not know the extent of my injuries and it was pretty clear that I wouldn't be able to make it out on my own the next day. I was airlifted from our camp by the Alaska National Guard (210th Div.) at 2200 and then flown to an Anchorage hospital. I was released from the hospital at 0600 (after a million x-rays) with only a few stitches in my knee and a bruised lower back.

Analysis

Kirk and I are experienced climbers, having climbed in Alaska for several years. In this instance, we let our guard down and failed to give the creek a wide enough berth in our haste to wrap up the climb and get out of the rain. We neglected to consider that the underlying terrain might differ from the fairly benign snow slope we were walking on. Narrow gullies and large terrain features can easily be hidden in the deep snows of the Chugach Mountains, and drifting on leeward slopes can fills gullies 50–70 feet deep. Kirk and I had ascended Cantata Peak by a different route and were unfamiliar with the path taken by the creek as it flows into the lower valley from the tarn. We didn't know of the waterfall as it was buried under the snowpack. Returning to the site of the accident four weeks later, we could see the twists and turns of the creek.

I found that had I been walking a mere four feet to the right, I would have been over solid ground and missed the waterfall completely. The terrain and snow conditions on the day of the accident were such that roped travel was completely unnecessary and would have been a hindrance. Had we been roped together, I might not have fallen down the waterfall. (Upon later inspection I found that I had broken through the snow about 15 feet upstream of the water-fall lip where the creek travels over extremely smooth rock at a 15-degree angle.) However, had we been roped, it's also possible I would have gotten stuck in the creek under the snowpack and would have drowned at the end of the rope before my partner could extricate me. (Crawling up the slippery rock with a pack on would probably have been impossible.)

I consider myself extremely lucky to have survived this accident at all. I could have easily drowned or sustained injuries in the fall that would have made it difficult or impossible to climb out under my own power. I attribute my survival to a bit of luck (I landed on my backpack which had enough gear in it to cushion the fall), a lot of willpower and adrenaline (I did NOT want to freeze to death), and to my cool-headed partner. Without his help, I probably wouldn't have been able to extricate myself from the waterfall-cave. I also firmly believe that my helmet saved my life. Had I not been wearing a helmet, it is likely that I would have been knocked unconscious in the fall and then would have drowned. I'm typically adamant about helmet-wearing when doing any form of climbing, but after this episode, it's the first thing I look for when packing and it never comes off until I'm near the car.

After the accident, Kirk and I decided that it was imperative that each part-ner carry a 40–50 foot piece of a small diameter (7mm) of rope as a safety line in the event of a similar accident where the victim has the rope (or loses it). It was fortunate for me that Kirk had 35 feet of webbing in the form of slings. I returned to the accident site on two occasions to examine the terrain as it came out from under the snow and to determine if my backpack could be recovered. I estimated that 50 feet of snow was in the gully beneath the waterfall at the time of the accident. On July 25 (six weeks later) there was still a large mass of snow 25 feet thick in the area below the waterfall. However, the snow had melted away from the rock to the point where it was relatively safe for me to rappel next to the waterfall to recover my pack that lay in a pool of water at the bottom. (Source: The victim)

PRE-EXISTING MEDICAL CONDITION—FAILURE TO INFORM GUIDES
Alaska, Mount McKinley, West Buttress

On June 16, John Cloe (59), a client of a guided Rainier Mountaineering, Inc., expedition began experiencing chest pain the late afternoon while climbing to the 14,200 foot camp. Upon arriving in camp at 1900, he told his guide, Gary Talcott, of the pain in his chest. Talcott took Cloe over to the Park Service Ranger Station, where Dr. Dudley Weider and Army Medic Raymond McPeek gave him a thorough exam at 2100. Cloe mentioned that he had experienced angina four or five years before, which he had not told the guide service. Weider and McPeek concurred that Cloe was experiencing angina and should be evacuated as soon as possible. At 2116, Ranger Roger Robinson called the Talkeetna Ranger Station to inform them of the situation. Weather on the lower glaciers was somewhat marginal for flying, while remaining good at 14,200 feet. The NPS LAMA helicopter departed Talkeetna at 2024 arriving at 14,200 feet at 2302. Cloe was flown straight to Talkeetna where he was met by the Talkeetna Ambulance Service at 2340. Cloe was transported by ambulance to Valley Hospital in Palmer.

Analysis

John Cloe would probably not have been permitted to join the guided party if he had disclosed his previous medical background. He put himself, the guides, and Park Service at risk because of his desire to climb Mount McKinley. Previous medical conditions should be seriously analyzed and disclosed before embarking on such endeavors. (Source: Roger Robinson, Mountaineering Ranger)

HAPE, ASCENDING TOO FAST, INADEQUATE FLUIDS
Alaska, Mount McKinley, West Buttress

On June 18, at 1030, Lucas Vidal Proveda, leader of the Spanish expedition Grup De Montanya, reported to Ranger Roger Robinson at the 14,200 foot camp on Mount McKinley that a member of his expedition was ill. Robinson proceeded to their camp, where he found Alvaro Fernandez Ferrer (25) experiencing severe High Altitude Pulmonary Edema. Ferrer was non-ambulatory, therefore he was sledded to the medical tent where he was treated by Dr. Dudley Weider and VIP Scott Darnsey (EMT-2). The initial assessment at 1041 indicated that Ferrer had an SPO_2 of 37, a pulse of 133 and respirations of 44. Both lungs were nearly full. He was put on oxygen and an IV was started. The Talkeetna Ranger Station was notified, and it was determined that Ferrer should be evacuated as soon as possible. At 1301 the NPS LAMA helicopter landed. Ferrer was flown to the 7,200 foot base camp, then transported by Alaska Air Guard Pavehawk helicopter straight to Alaska Regional Hospital in Anchorage.

Analysis

Ferrer and his party took just four days to reach the 14,200 foot camp. Ferrer admitted to drinking very little over the prior 24 hours. Lack of fluids and their fast pace directly contributed to the HAPE. (Source: Roger Robinson, Mountaineering Ranger)

(Editor's Note: There was another HAPE incident this year. On the same day as above, a Japanese climber came into the 14,200 foot camp complaining of HAPE symptoms. This climber did not ascend too fast, but his age—58—and a detected heart murmur indicated a rapid helicopter evacuation.)

FALL ON SNOW, EXCEEDING ABILITIES, ASCENDING TOO FAST
Alaska, Mount McKinley, West Rib

A ten-member British Army expedition "Summit to the Sea" checked into the Talkeetna Ranger Station for their briefing on June 2. Their original plan was to ascend the West Buttress, which they had changed to doing the upper West

Rib, assessed as an Alaska Grade 4. The Park Service recommended they stay to the West Buttress (Grade 2), since several members had very little glacier or ice climbing experience. They would make their decision once they reached 14,200 feet on the West Buttress. The expedition departed Talkeetna on June 4. On June 14, nine members moved into the 14,200 foot camp. One member had returned to base camp a few days earlier. They acclimatized three days at 14,200 feet before ascending to a 16,200 foot camp on June 17. Ranger Roger Robinson at the 14,200 foot camp recommended that they take one or two rest days at 16,200 feet before making their summit attempt. At 0630 on June 18, the expedition departed for the summit.

Upon departing that morning, member Gary Keep experienced signs of AMS. The other eight members continued ascending while Keep soloed back to 14,200 feet. Keep was examined by Scott Darnsey of the Ranger Patrol, where it was determined that Keep was experiencing AMS and dehydration. Keep was admitted into the medical tent at 1530, where he was administered oxygen, Diamox, and an IV. His condition improved, and he was released at 2400 on June 18.

The other members continued an extremely slow ascent up through the rocks of the upper Rib. By 1830, they had reached 19,000 feet, having only ascended 2,800 feet in twelve hours. Weather conditions remained good throughout the day. The first team of three, led by Martin Spooner (33), decided to deviate to the right of the normal route where a break in the Football Field cornice was found. This break could be attained by first ascending a 45–50-degree hard snow slope which led up to a 20-foot corniced section of ice that topped out onto the Football Field.

Spooner was in the lead with Phil Whitfield (?) second and Steve Brown (25) third as they approached the cornice at 19,300 feet. At 1920, Brown lost his footing and fell, pulling Whitfield and Spooner with him. They tumbled approximately 300 feet before being stopped by large rocks. These rocks prevented an 8,000 foot fall off the south face. The other two rope teams were approximately 30 meters lateral of the team that fell and were resting when the accident occurred.

Spooner sustained injuries to both his ankles, while Whitfield received lacerations to his head. Brown received head injuries and was suffering from severe shock, delirium, and lapses of consciousness. The leader of the expedition, Justin Featherstone (29), attempted to call the Ranger Camp with their CB radio, but found that their batteries were too weak. Featherstone decided that he and Bougard would stay behind with Spooner and Brown and wait for a helicopter rescue. The other four, including Whitfield, would descend to 14,200 feet to report the accident. The four remaining each had bivi bags, down jacket, one shovel, one stove, one liter of fuel, and one day's food. They dug into the ice and built a small trench below several large rocks. This gave them some protection, but after the first night, they were unable to relight their stove due to the cold and windy conditions.

At 2030, the other four, including Whitfield, Johny Johnston, Ian Hayward and Nigel Coar, began their descent. They reached their 16,200 foot camp at 0030 on June 19. Hayward and Coar decided to stay at their camp while Whitfield and Johnston continued on down. At 0040, Whitfield and Johnston witnessed two Americans fall down the 45 degree snow slope on the West Rib known as the "Orient Express," coming to a stop at 15,800 feet. Whitfield and Johnston arrived at the accident scene at 0100 and provided assistance to the fallen Americans. Whitfield stayed behind with the Americans while Johnston decided to solo down for help. At 0220 Johnston reported both accidents to the 14,200 foot ranger camp. The Talkeetna Ranger Station was notified of the situation at 0240.

Weather conditions remained poor for a helicopter evacuation. A large ground team was assembled, first to evacuate the two Americans who were closer and more exposed. Once this was completed, a second plan would be developed to evacuate the British. During the American evacuation, Keep was escorted to his 16,200 foot camp with an NPS radio establishing a radio link from the ridge.

Brown's condition was deteriorating, so Featherstone decided the four would slowly begin their descent. All four attempted to descend, but Spooner experienced too much pain in his ankles to walk. Featherstone decided to take Brown down, leaving Bougard behind with Spooner. The foursome had only one rope, since their third rope had been damaged in the fall, so Spooner and Bougard opted to wait to be rescued. Unknown to Featherstone was the rescue operation of the Americans below his position. Weather at the 14,000-foot level and above began to improve so that at 1600, all four of the British climbers were observed through a spotting scope from the Ranger Camp. Shortly thereafter, Featherstone and Brown were observed descending. Brown was very unstable, requiring a constant belay and occasionally taking short falls. Weather improved enough to evacuate one of the Americans at 2230 by helicopter. At the same time, the two British were descending the "Orient Express," very close to where the Americans had fallen. At 2300 Featherstone and Brown fell 1,500 feet, ending where the Americans had landed at 15,800 feet. Featherstone had later commented that Brown had fallen into him, knocking him off his stance.

At 2300, Keep radioed from his 16,200-foot location to the Ranger Cap that they had witnessed the fall and would be providing assistance. Ranger staff also witnessed the fall. Plans were developed for their evacuation. Featherstone had broken his left leg in the fall, while Brown sustained additional head injuries. Brown was able to walk and decided to descend straight down the route to the 14,200-foot camp for help.

Brown's descent was observed from the 14,200-foot camp. It was apparent his judgment was impaired. A well marked trail led from their accident location to 14,200 feet, but Brown's decision to descend a direct course would lead him over an ice cliff and several crevasses. Brown was observed walking straight off a 20-foot ice cliff, then tumbling down a steep slope where he was buried in avalanche debris. He freed himself from the debris, then continued his descent. Not 30 seconds later he was observed falling into a crevasse. Brown recalled that he attempted to climb 30 feet out, clawing with bare fingers and kicking with his crampons. Brown had lost his ice ax on one of his earlier falls, then lost his gloves on the fall down the Orient. After 30 minutes and several attempts, Brown clawed his way out to where he lay motionless by the lip of the crevasse. Eventually he stood up. Ascending rescuers shouted to Brown to stay put.

Because of Spooner's and Bougard's position at 19,000 feet, and the fact that all able bodied rescuers at 14,200 feet had exhausted themselves over two long nights of rescues, the shorthaul extraction became the more logical choice of getting them off if the weather cooperated. When the weather began to improve on the evening of June 21, Jay Hudson was able to spot the pair at 2035, where they were standing and waving, to everyone's relief. Establishing a good communication link with the pair was imperative in order to perform this shorthaul mission. The initial cargo drop of radio and survival gear established this communication link. Once we could talk with the pair, we could judge their physical and mental capabilities, and get current weather conditions. The pair had previous training using a similar "Screamer Suit" (big diaper) in the military. This allowed the two to be extracted without a ranger involved in the shorthaul. Weather was the primary factor in retrieving both at the same time, since conditions were constantly changing for the worse. This had been the first time in many days that the upper mountain was calm. At 0248 on June 22, the LAMA helicopter held a hover at maximum power until the two were hooked in. Then a slow descent was made directly to the Ranger Camp. At this point the LAMA had to refuel at 7,200 feet then return. When the LAMA came back into 14,200 feet, the weather was already changing and it was fortunate that the pair got flown off. This shorthaul performed may be the highest shorthaul rescue mission ever performed in the world. Pilot Jim Hood did an exceptional job in the decreased light and high altitude conditions.

Analysis

Here is a good example of an inexperienced party getting in over their heads by attempting too difficult a route. The "Summit to the Sea" expedition was advised in Talkeetna to stay on the West Buttress since half the party had very little glacier or ice climbing experience. While at 14,200 feet, they were advised to take several days to acclimatize at their high camp, since their summit day would be a long one. Because of good weather, they chose to make their summit push the next morning. Their lack of acclimatization became apparent when one member became ill on summit day and the rest required twelve hours to ascend just 2,800 feet over technically easy ground. The experienced members in the party should have realized that their slow pace was a good indication that it was time to turn around. To make matters worse, after a long day they planned to attempt a difficult corniced finish to the West Rib—a route seldom tried even by very experienced parties. On top of all these concerns they left an ill member behind in camp, who was then forced to solo down because of his AMS. To further their predicament, the leader descended with a person who was unstable, down a route notorious for its falls. Belays and fixed protection should have been used. The leader was familiar with the route and conditions they had ascended the day before, which would have been the safer choice. Had they carried extra batteries for their radio, the pair could have been warned about the conditions in the descent route.

The two who survived four nights out in bivi bags were incredibly lucky. A strong will and determination kept them alive. (Source: Roger Robinson, Mountaineering Ranger.

FALL ON ICE, UNABLE TO SELF-ARREST, INADEQUATE BELAY
Alaska, Mount McKinley, West Buttress
William Finley (24) and Jeff Munroe (25) were injured in a 2,000 foot fall down the "Orient Express" section of the West Rib route on Mount McKinley June 18 at 0040. Both were descending roped together when they slipped on 45-degree ice around 17,800 feet, ending their fall at the 15,800 foot level. Finley sustained chest injuries while Munroe was knocked unconscious. Both men were lowered down to the Ranger Camp by a rescue team. Munroe remained unconscious through his evacuation on June 19. Finley was evacuated on June 21 by an Army Chinook helicopter. Both were transported to Alaska Regional Hospital in Anchorage.
Analysis
Billy Finley and Jeff Munroe were the eighteenth and nineteenth climbers to have fallen down the Orient Express. They were only the third and fourth to have survived. They were very lucky the two British climbers witnessed the fall and could immediately provide assistance. The quick responses from Johnston, Whitfield, 14K rescuers, the NPS LAMA, and the 14K medical attention certainly saved their lives. (Source: Roger Robinson, Mountaineering Ranger)

HAND-HOLD CAME LOOSE, FALL ON ROCK, PLACED NO PROTECTION
California, Yosemite Valley
On January 26, Katherine Davis (31) was climbing on Supplication (5.10). She was leading a 5.8 approach to set a belay at a ledge when the rock handhold she was holding crumbled off the wall. At the time of the fall Davis was wearing a seat harness with gear, but was not clipped through any protection. Eric Pearlman, her partner, said that Davis pitched out and back as she fell, rotating 360 degrees head over heels. They estimated the fall to be between 25 and 30 feet. Davis fell onto a steep granite slope covered with heavy duff and soil. She landed on her feet and left side, then slid another 20 feet down a steep soil slope missing the talus. Pearlman stated that he was sure Davis had not lost consciousness because he heard her say, "I'm OK, I'm OK," as she slid down the slope. After checking on Davis' condition, Pearlman hiked out and reported the incident to Yosemite Dispatch, using the phone at the Arch Rock Entrance. Ranger Carol Mutch was the station attendant at the time. After making his report, he returned to Davis' location to await rescue crews.

She was placed in a full body splint which was secured in a litter. A litter carry out team was assembled and, using several belay systems, the litter was carried down approximately ¼ mile of talus slope to Hwy 140. Although the air ambulance was ordered, it was later canceled and Davis was taken by ground ambulance to the Yosemite Medical Clinic where she was treated for a green-stick fracture of the pelvis and released. (Source: Ruth Middlecamp, Ranger, Yosemite National Park.)

Analysis
The first 50 feet of this route is rotten (loose) rock, with lousy protection pos-sibilities, so the standard practice is to free-solo that part before setting up a belay anchor. We don't know whether she tested the hold. She leads hard routes and is comfortable free-soloing 5.9. (Source: John Dill, SAR Ranger, Yosemite National Park)

EXPOSURE TO SEVERE WEATHER, HYPOTHERMIA, INADEQUATE EQUIP-MENT—PORTALEDGE, POOR POSITION
California, Yosemite Valley, El Capitan

On May 26 at 1415, Yosemite Dispatch received a telephone call from Robert Burton, who reported that he had received a cellular telephone call from Craig Calonica (45), who, along with Jordi Tosas (30) was climbing "New Dawn" on El Capitan. Calonica asked Burton to call the Park and summon help for Tosas. According to Calonica, Tosas was hypothermic and in "pretty bad shape" after spending the night "sitting in a waterfall" inside his portaledge. Tosas' single, A-5 portaledge fly system was inadequate against the snow/rain storm they experienced the night before. Calonica did not believe Tosas would make it through another night without suffering severe hypothermia.

A rescue effort was immediately initiated to remove Tosas from El Capitan before nightfall. A two-pronged strategy was developed. First, fly the rescue team to the top of El Capitan to implement a raising/lowering system; second, fly a helicopter with winch capability to remove Tosas from the wall. Tosas was removed using the throw bag technique and winch from Naval Air Station Leemore.

Calonica was raised to the top of El Capitan by the rope rescue team. By 2030, all rescue personnel and both climbers were returned to the heli-base. Tosas was transported to Yosemite Medical Clinic for medical observation. (Source: Ruth Middlecamp, Ranger, Yosemite National Park)

Analysis
Calonica had a cell phone, lap top, e-mail setup and a weather radio, yet he said the storm was a complete surprise. Tosas is a very experienced interna-tional climber and UIAGM guide. Tosas' portaledge was an older style and not adequate for the conditions, especially in the location where it was pitched. Here is part of a transcript from an interview with Craig Calonica:

"We were both getting wet, damp, but not really soaked. We were sitting on the ledge under the fly, getting condensation on us where we touched the fly. We sat there for quite a while, waiting for it to stop. We didn't want to break out the other ledge because we thought it was going to blow through and we weren't planning to stay there.

"That's when I called a friend in the Bay Area and he said it was clear and should be clearing up in the Valley soon, but it didn't look like it to me... I've lived at Squaw my entire life and we'll be getting a blizzard when it's clear in the Bay.

"The next morning (Tuesday) it was cold as hell. Every bit of water froze when it touched something. That's when I noticed, speaking with Jordi, that he was having problems, chattering, couldn't do simple functions like grabbing gear from the bag, like clothes, food, an extra ensolite pad. He had all the bags under him.

"I was doing fine. I had all my gear in my ledge before I got in and I changed into my Gorctcx one-piccc suit. This was Monday evening about five. I left everything on. If there was a break I was going to go on.

"In the morning we were getting hit hard first by rain, then it broke up and was clear, steamy on the wall, but bitter cold and windy. And the runoff was turning to ice. There were icicles hanging off my ropes above us and I knew we'd get nailed when the ice above us started releasing. I remember big [sheets of ice] coming of Zenyatta a few years ago. Even though the wall was steep, they were flying back into the wall. So I was looking at the ice above us and thinking this was not a good situation, with it cold like this. More than anything else it was bitter cold. I can't remember it being that cold that time of year, ever.

"I wanted to move out of there, but I knew Jordi wasn't in any shape to go. Our bags were brand new Moonstone dri-loft Goretex. If you sit inside those things they're going to keep you warm no matter what, even if you're soaking wet. Mine *was* soaking wet—I could have sponged it out. Jordi's was the same. He said he had a river going through his ledge, big gushes of water at times.

"Everything in my ledge was soaking wet but I had no rivers, just condensation. I stuck some things out late that day to try to get them to drip dry, but they froze solid instantly.

"My ledge was an A5/North Face double and the fly had a tent pole that kept the fly off of me—a great thing to have. It was a standard fly. Jordi had my single A5 ledge, an older model, with a seam-sealed fly, like brand new. Mine was not seam sealed, but it had only one seam." (Source: From a report by John Dill, SAR, Yosemite National Park)

STRANDED, INEXPERIENCE, INADEQUATE CLOTHING, DARKNESS, WEATHER
California, Yosemite Valley, Royal Arches
On May 28, Kevin Calvert (18) and Kacee Fujinami (19) were benighted while descending Royal Arches. They were able to complete the descent early the next morning, though a rescue effort had been put in place.
Analysis
This seemingly bland incident has some interesting lessons. Below is a summary of information provided to rangers in an interview.

Experience. Kacee Fujinami and Calvert were here in Yosemite with the Alpine Club of Santa Maria High School. Both were acting as advisors with the club. Both were described by the RP as the most experienced climbers in the club. Kacee Fujinami's (19) climbing experience has been predominantly in sport climbing, describing herself as a YDS 5.9 sport climber. Fujinami has no traditional lead climbing experience. The longest route climbed prior to this was a five pitch route that she seconded.

Kevin Calvert (18) stated that he had five years of climbing experience and that he climbs at least one day a week. Calvert describes himself as leading "hard" 5.10 traditional routes. The longest route Calvert has climbed is the East Buttress of Middle Cathedral Rock. Calvert stated that he has climbed at least one other route of similar difficulty and length in the Needles.

Clothing. Fujinami wore light cotton pants, a cotton t-shirt, a light cotton long underwear shirt, a light cotton sweatshirt, and a nylon shell jacket (untreated, non-waterproof, not a Goretex type fabric). Fujinami had no hat or gloves. Fujinami had no wind pants or rain pants. Calvert wore a cotton t-shirt, a cotton long underwear shirt and a medium weight synthetic pile top. Calvert did not have a rain jacket or rain pants. Calvert wore a leather sun shade type hat. Calvert did not have a wind breaker, rain parka, or rain pants.

Equipment. Fujinami and Calvert carried one pack between them that contained an EMS type emergency space blanket and a light plastic poncho, four or five one-liter bottles of water, and they had one head lamp and a flashlight. They climbed with two 11mm, 165 foot, dynamic climbing ropes. They carried a rack that included SLCD, tricams, wired nuts, quick draws and slings.

The Climb. Fujinami and Calvert began the climb at 0830 following a last minute decision to do this climb rather than what had been planned earlier—that being to do shorter routes with the other members of their club. Fujinami and Calvert planned to descend the bolted rappel route. Neither was familiar with the North Dome Gully descent other than knowing it existed.

Calvert did all of the leading. They were aware of the weather report and that rain was forecast for the afternoon, having been advised of that at the Mountain Shop in Curry Village just prior to leaving that morning. Calvert stated that he expected to climb the route in four or five hours.

As they reached the top of the tenth pitch around 1630, it began to rain. They decided to rappel. On the first rappel, Calvert threw the ropes down and began the rappel using an ATC as a brake. Calvert rappelled less than 50 feet when he discovered the ropes entangled but not stuck below him.

Calvert stated that he was on a blank slab without convenient ledges. He attempted to pull up a bight of rope and tie himself off with it so that he might safely use both hands to untangle the two ropes, but was unsuccessful in achieving this. He then reascended the rope 50 feet to the ledge where he began his rappel. He did this by levering up on the climbing rope and locking off on the ATC. He pulled the entangled rappel ropes back up to the ledge, sorted them out, and redeployed them. Calvert was apparently unfamiliar with the prusik technique.

Fujinami and Calvert made a total of four rappels before dark, stopping on a large ledge system on the normal route, about 200 feet above the ground. They spent the night huddled together wrapped in the poncho and space blanket at this location. The weather conditions were extreme, with high winds, heavy snow/sleet and 30 degree temperatures.

In conclusion, there are some key points to keep in mind. 1) Royal Arches is a 17 pitch route rated at the YDS 5.7 A1 level, and is well described in the first chapter, "Staying Alive," of the guide book they had. The specific problems they encountered are discussed. 2) Their clothing choice needs no further comment. 3) They did not adhere to a turn-around time. 4) Not knowing how to prusik resulted in taking more time to untangle the ropes. 5) By tying their two ropes together, they could have made a single rappel to the ground from the ledge where they bivouacked. (Source: From Yosemite National Park Case Incident Reports)

FALL ON ROCK, EQUIPMENT FAILURE—CARABINER BROKE
California, Lover's Leap

Gear worries were far from our minds on a beautiful June morning when Tom Stargaard and I were heading off to Lovers Leap for a day of climbing. The recent cover photo on *Climbing Magazine* had renewed our interest in this fine area, and we hoped to spend the day climbing a few of the classics.

A trio of climbers was completing The Groove, but since they appeared to be setting up a top rope, we decided we would also have to forgo this last of the classic pitches on the Lower Buttress. After passing The Farce, we looked over at a steep crack that we had known about for a few years, but had never actually climbed. It was reputed to be a short, awkward 5.10a/b crack that lacked character. After a brief discussion, we decided that, since neither one of us had ever done this route, we might as well give it a go.

Despite the fact that I had been climbing much more than usual for the past few weeks, I was "sketchy" as I led up the first pitch. In my customary fashion, I placed several pieces of gear—a small Camalot right off the ground, an old hex just above. At the first 5.10 section, I placed a wire and a TCU. Higher, another wire and another TCU. As I reached a bulge, about twenty feet off the ground, I stepped up onto a face hold and placed a beautiful number 3.5 Camalot. I clipped the attached "hot wire" carabiner and was relieved to be to the hand crack. I pulled the bulge and continued up the crack. About five feet higher, I placed a number 3 Camalot, carefully clipping the color coordinated blue anodized Quicksilver " 'biner." Just above this, the crack pinched off with a horizontal dike—a frequent characteristic of Lovers Leap climbs. As I contemplated this move, I felt a little shaky, but I knew that I had protection at my knee, and once I pulled past this section, I would be on easier ground. While I was trying to decide if I should pull on the dike or crank from an insecure hand jam, I came off. I did, however, have time to warn my belayer. Tom braced for what he thought would be a short fall.

As I dropped, it seemed to me that the piece at my knee pulled rather easily. In apparent slow motion, I flipped upside down and rapidly approached the ground, head first and backwards. Finally, with an abrupt, yet springy halt, I stopped just short of the rocks and brush at the base of the wall. Just as the rope pulled tight, the back of my head smacked against the granite, and blood shot out in abundance. I had an incredible rush of adrenaline and a hollow feeling in the pit of my stomach; I was shaking all over. Tom yelled, "Are you okay?" I quickly flipped onto my feet and realized that, other than the hole in my head, I was actually okay. I did, however, have some kind of strange sympathetic neck sensation, knowing that if I had gone six inches further, I would have snapped my neck.

I tried to untie from the harness, but the knot had pulled so tight I couldn't get it undone. Thomas volunteered to run down to the other climbers to get a knife. Before he left, he gave me his T-shirt to help slow the profusion of blood from my head. While Thomas was gone, I looked for my glasses that dropped during the fall. I saw them, but didn't retrieve them right away. I continued to fiddle with the knot; soon Thomas was back and we cut the rope. At this point, I walked over to the base of the climb, took out the first piece of gear I had placed, picked up the rack, looked up at the wall and noticed that, strangely, the rope was not running through the number 3 Camalot. Rather, it was five feet lower through the 3.5 Camalot. However, the higher number 3 Camalot, the piece that was at knee level when I fell, was still in place. Confused, I put on my glasses and continued down the trail.

I was feeling well enough where we opted not to drive to the hospital in Tahoe. Instead we headed towards home in Auburn. Within two hours of taking the fall, I was in a small office with a doctor and three nurses. They shaved part of my head, injected anesthetics and cleansers directly into the wound, and ultimately sewed me up with eight stitches, telling me the whole time how lucky I was. Meanwhile, I continued to replay the events of the morning in my mind, always wondering, how did the rope come unclipped from the blue carabiner?

Analysis

For the next several days, I hung around my house thinking about climbing. I spent a lot of time on the phone with friends who called to offer their condolences, express their happiness that I was okay, and ask what had happened. I decided that the following Tuesday I would return to Lovers Leap, pick up the gear that I had left, and go climbing to see how it felt to be out on the sharp end once again. After my fall, we had arranged with Brent and Steve, the two friendly climbers with the knife, to remove my gear from the climb and leave it at Strawberry Lodge for me to pick up later. When I walked into the lodge, the day manager, Mary, greeted us. As she handed me the gear, I was shocked to discover that the blue Quicksilver carabiner that had been clipped to the number 3 Camalot was actually broken in two. In over thirty years of climbing I had not seen or heard of a 'biner actually breaking in a "routine" fall; I was stunned. Climbing gear just doesn't break. When I later talked to both Steve and Brent they relayed how when Steve had rappelled the route to clean the gear, he was horrified to come to a Camalot with a broken 'biner hanging limply from the sling. The two climbers sat at the base of the climb pondering, "How did that guy break a carabiner?"

I am happy to report that I put the broken carabiner in the trunk, grabbed the rest of my gear, and we headed off for a great day of climbing at Lovers Leap. I did, of course, wear my helmet, and it was amazing the sense of comfort that I had.

I learned a great deal from this experience. First, it is my intention to always climb with a helmet. A beautiful, sunny day, as we've learned many times from all sorts of climbing literature, can quickly turn to tragedy. A helmet offers peace of mind and protection. Second, I've learned that gear does break. Just because the pro is at your knee and the wall is smooth and steep, doesn't mean that the system is fool proof. After hours of discussing this issue with friends—fellow climbers with literally hundreds of years of combined experience—we've concluded that there's not enough in the journals about the whiplash phenomena of carabiners. During the course of a fall, a carabiner can snap open. If during the instant that the gate is open, the climber's full weight comes on the 'biner, it can snap, as probably happened in my case. Rod Johnson, designer of the Bod Harness, modifier of the original Chouinard stopper, and five year employee of Chouinard Equipment analyzed the carabiner and said that it showed all the classic signs of being loaded with the gate open. After talking on the phone to Black Diamond's Quality Assurance Manager, Chris Harmston, I agreed to send him the broken binder and a few others of similar type and age. After testing and inspecting my gear, he also concluded that "the carabiner struck the rock during the impact of the fall and caused the gate to open due to whiplash." The odds of this are very slim, but it did happen to me.

Third, check the gate open strength of your carabiners. Common industry practice is to prominently display the open and closed KN rating of the carabiner. I am currently upgrading my carabiners to an open gate KN rating of, at least, nine. (A KN is a force or impact rating. One KN is approximately 225 lbs.)

Fourth, my experience also reconfirmed the fact that dogged insistence on anchoring the belay is essential. Tom was tethered to a tree, and it helped him stop me just in time. It also convinced me that placing a lot of protection is a good idea. For years when I have been climbing, I wonder, "what happens if this piece fails?" Well, now I know, it can happen, and it's good to have another piece not too far away.

Fifth, after ignoring or only half-heartedly understanding all the information about UIAA ratings and statistics, I have a vivid example of how a short fall near the ground can create a huge amount of force, because there is so little rope out to absorb the impact. I now carry some lightweight, locking carabiners on my rack to help stem the whiplash effect when leading difficult pitches near the ground. I have been told that a number of climbers have been doing this for years; I just never noticed the practice. Most of my new, replacement 'biners are the type with wire gates. They have a greater open gate test strength, and the wire gate is less prone to whiplash.

Finally, climbers, check your gear! (Source: Bart O'Brien)

FALL ON ICE, WEATHER, EXCEEDING ABILITIES
California, Mount Shasta
On June 25, Lois Johnson (52) and her husband Tom had camped at Lake Helen and were climbing the standard Avalanche Glacier route when she lost her balance while putting on dark glasses as the sun rose. She was just 50 vertical feet from the security of Red Banks, a recommended resting point before continuing to the summit (14,162 feet). The surface was hard ice over snow, caused by a freezing rain on the night before the climb. Lois rocketed down the 35-degree ice slope, ice ax jerked from her gloveless hands, and came to a stop in old avalanche debris 2000 feet below. One boot with crampon attached was torn off and the other ankle was badly fractured. Lois and Tom and a solo climber, who had turned back, were the only ones attempting the summit that morning. The solo climber descended to find a cell phone two hours distant. Tom assisted his wife using their down jackets and extra clothing. After three hours, they were joined on the icy slope by two doctors who were camped at Lake Helen and a bivy equipped climber. Lois was warmed and stabilized until a military helicopter rescue could be effected when the cloud cover broke just before nightfall.
Analysis
Lois and Tom had discussed ice ax arrest techniques the night before, but they had not practiced arrests. Self-belay techniques were not reviewed. Lois had taken the one-day snow travel orientation with Rainier Mountaineering, Inc. in a previous year but had not climbed with Tom. Tom had completed several guided climbs, including Mt. Shasta, two years previously. A recent snow climb up South Sister, the guided climbs and five years hiking and scrambling experience had not prepared Lois and Tom for the dangerous conditions of high cold winds, hard ice and a 35-degree slope. (Source: Robert Speik)

STRANDED, OFF ROUTE, INEXPERIENCE
California, Yosemite Valley, Royal Arches
On July 8 around 2330, Yosemite dispatch received multiple 911 calls reporting cries for help coming from the wall near the Awahnee hotel. Ranger Keith Lober investigated and found two climbers calling for help above the Bathtub on the "Royal Arches" descent route. Upon arrival at the Bathtub, Lober found one climber stuck at the end of his rappel rope about 30 feet from the ground. The second climber was secure on a ledge above.

At 2345 an SAR page went out and a team of five rescuers responded. Rescuers climbed up to the stranded climber, placed anchors, and assisted him to the ground. One rescuer then continued up to the second climber and, due to the climber's inexperience, set up a system to lower him to the ground. All personnel were clear of the field by 0300 on July 9.
Analysis
Once on the ground the climbers were interviewed and provided the following information: Lead climber Jason Mathew (22) has been climbing for three to four years and usually climbs five times a week, including bouldering. He can

lead up to a 5.8 traditional and has completed ten multi-pitch climbs such as the "Crack" and the "Nutcracker." Partner Dan Pier (25) was on his first multi-pitch climb and had completed just a few short practice climbs up to a 5.8 difficulty. Mathew and Pier had started the climb around 0800 and one other team had passed them during the day. Mathew had read "Staying Alive in Yosemite" by John Dill. As a note, Mathew was carrying enough equipment to have completed a self-rescue by a variety of methods. (Source: J. Pederson and K. Lober, Rangers, Yosemite National Park)

RAPPELLED OFF END OF ROPE—FALL ON ROCK, MISCALCULATED RAPPEL STATION
California, Yosemite Valley, El Capitan

On July 13, as we were preparing to start the Shield route in Yosemite, California, I (Matthew Luck) was ascending the fifth fixed (static) line from the ground up to Heart Ledge on El Capitan, while my partner, Steve Canavero, waited at the anchor below. He was standing on a fairly substantial ledge (one meter wide) which angled off on the side for about ten meters before dropping vertically.

As I was jugging, Eric Renger, was rappelling down from Heart Ledge on the dynamic lead line he and his partner, David Hill, had just fixed. They had just climbed the Free Blast up to Mammoth Terraces and rappelled to Heart Ledge, intending to fix those pitches and begin the Salathé Wall the next day.

When I was about two-thirds of the way to the anchor above, there was this commotion, and I looked down to see Eric fall and hit the top of the sloping part of the ledge. There was a loud crashing as he landed on his garbage bag full of empty water bottles. He then began to slide down the ledge to the edge where it drops off (which would have resulted in a four-pitch fall to the ground). Clawing at the crack where the ledge meets the wall, he slid about three meters, gaining no purchase in the crack.

All of a sudden, the sliding climber came to a stop. Simultaneously, my rope dropped about two meters. I had no idea what was going on at the moment, and yelled, "Hey, what are you doing up there?" thinking that his partner (still at the anchor above) was somehow undoing the anchor of the fixed line I was ascending.

Eric yelled, "I'm OK, but I don't know what's holding me!" Steve then yelled for no one to move, thinking that a stuck rope had somehow stopped his fall and a move by anyone could have dislodged it and he would have continued falling off of the large flake.

A few moments later, everything was still, and we began to figure out what had happened. Steve then pulled slack up from the other static rope Eric was trailing (he had two) and threw the end to him. Eric was positioned precariously in the crack and was obviously worried about the mystery that held him. He questioned the integrity of the rope anchor at least twice, and Steve assured him it was solid and backed it up with a figure-8 on a bight.

As things calmed down, I finished jugging up to Heart Ledge, and told his partner what had happened. There are two fixed anchors at the Heart Ledges area, one at Heart Ledge and one below Heart Ledge, and these are about six meters apart vertically. The other party had fixed their rope and rappelled from the higher anchor, and their rope ended up about five meters short of the next rappel station. He rappelled to the station six meters below, fixed his line there, and then rappelled to his partner, who had sustained no major injuries. (Source: Matthew Luck)

Analysis

I rappelled first, as Dave waited, clipped into the anchors on Heart Ledge. As I started the rappel, I couldn't see to the next anchor, and I didn't know if the 50 m rope would reach all the way. About 30 feet down from the Heart Ledge rappel anchor, I saw another bolted rappel anchor.

Seeing another anchor partway down the rappel made me think we might need to set up another rappel to reach the next rappel station below. I didn't have any solid information on exactly which rappel anchors to use, and I have been on more than a few rappel routes that had extra rappel anchors. I mentioned the extra rappel anchor to Dave, and continued to rappel.

As I often do on walls, I had a prusik knot on the rappel rope above my HB Sheriff belay device. There were not any knots in the end of the rappel rope, which is also how I normally choose to rappel. I had my ascenders set up and clipped to my harness, so I could easily and safely ascend the rope if I needed to return to the lower rappel anchor.

Initially, I thought the rappel anchor had failed, or the rappel rope had broken. However, as I looked up, I could see the end of my rappel rope dangling 20 feet above the lower rappel anchors. I had simply rappelled off the end of my rope, which was too short to reach from Heart Ledge to the next rappel station. Steve was still waiting at the lower rappel anchors, which were now above me and to the right. I asked him to set up a fixed rope so that I could safely anchor to something and then ascend back to the ledge. I knew that the ropes I had been trailing had somehow caught me, but I didn't know how they held me. After Steve fixed my trailing rope for me, I checked several times to make sure I was on the correct rope, and that it was securely anchored. Once I was sure it was safe, I jumarred back up the ramp to the ledge, pulling a mess of ropes with me.

Once I got up onto the ledge, I clipped to the anchors and sat down to rest. Dave soon rappelled down to where I was, and we talked over what had happened. I had clearly rappelled off the end of the rappel line, and the prusik knot did nothing to stop me. It was my trailing ropes, which had become tangled with the fixed rope, that saved my life. One end of the trailing rope was attached to my harness. As I tumbled down the ramp, I grabbed the free end of my trailing rope. The middle of my trailing rope was looped over the fixed rope, and this is what stopped my fall. Because the fixed rope was attached to rappel anchors at both ends, the full length of my trailing rope was being pulled up over the fixed rope as I tumbled down the ramp. As I soon as I grabbed the free end of the trailing rope, I was essentially belaying myself on the trailing rope, with the fixed rope as my top-rope anchor.

My injuries from the fall were pretty minor. I had a bad bruise for several weeks from landing on the ledge, and I got bad rope burns on two fingers from grabbing the ropes.

In the seven years that I've been climbing, I hadn't made any serious mistakes on the rock or had any close calls. As I sat on the ledge, I realized that I couldn't say that anymore. I'd read plenty of accident reports and advice for safe climbing. I knew that many accidents occurred when experienced climbers stopped paying attention and made a mistake. But now, I was one of those climbers, and it made me feel a lot more vulnerable, and a lot less secure on the rock. I don't like thinking about the accident too much, especially when I consider all the "what if" scenarios and resulting consequences.

After letting things settle down for a while on the ledge, Dave and I continued to rappel to the ground, and Steve and Matt continued up to Heart Ledge. Dave and I didn't finish the Salathé route that week, but we did spend the week climbing other free routes in Yosemite, and we plan to return to the Salathé some day. (Source: Eric Renger)

FALL ON ROCK, PROTECTION PULLED OUT—INADEQUATE
California, Yosemite Valley

On September 6, David Craig (32) first met and climbed with a Japanese climber named Tomo (last name unknown). Tomo was experienced and competent. On Sunday they climbed at the base of Sunnyside Bench.

After climbing a few other short routes, Craig decided to lead Lingering Lie (5.10). The route followed an under-climb that curved up to the right and then curved to the left. Craig placed his first piece of protection, a Camalot, about ten feet off the ground, then climbed another eight feet or so into the crux section and placed a second Camalot. This placement was blind; that is, he was unable to see into the crack to evaluate the reliability of the placement. He attached a two foot sling to the piece, clipped in the rope, and climbed until the piece was a couple of feet below his feet.

The climbing seemed harder than the rating at this point. He knew he was going to fall and called out, "Take," to his belayer to warn Tomo to take in any existing slack rope. But he fell before Tomo could act. He fell about eight feet, saw the Camalot stem shift downward before it failed. He fell about 15 feet to the ground. He landed on his feet on a small patch of dirt, doubled up and rocked forward, striking his face with his knee, then pitched backwards, landing hard on the rock with his butt.

He knew he was hurt, and nearby climbers checked him over while others went for help. At the clinic he was found to have a fractured left calcaneous, a fractured coccyx, and a lacerated knee (from his teeth).

Analysis

David Craig had been climbing actively for six years on traditional rock routes, leads 5.10 comfortably, is competent at placing and judging protection, has taken lots of falls, but has no previous climbing injuries or rescues. He is familiar with Yosemite granite, having climbed approximately 50 routes in the park on this and one previous trip.

Craig's belayer might have shortened his fall by taking in slack, but he had no time to do so. Craig feels he should have placed protection a few feet before (lower than) the piece that failed. He could see the crack there and could have placed a reliable piece that would have kept him off the ground. (Source: John Dill, SAR Ranger, Yosemite National Park)

FALL ON ROCK, INADEQUATE BELAY—ROPE TOO SHORT and NO KNOT IN END
California, Yosemite National Park, Guppy Dome

On September 7, Scott Davidson (54) led a short pitch, fixed an anchor and had his belayer lower him (with an ATC). The rope (50m) was too short for the task and there was no safety knot in the end. The end of the rope ran through the ATC and Davidson fell 15 feet to a ledge, then 30 feet on a slab, spraining his ankle. (Source: John Dill and Martin Ziebell, SAR Rangers, Yosemite National Park)

(Editor's Note: One of many incidents of this kind for the year. By the end of this book, the reader will wonder if some kind of short rope, no knots, etc., epidemic struck the climbing scene this year.)

FALL ON ROCK, INADEQUATE PROTECTION—PULLED OUT
California, Yosemite Valley, El Capitan

On September 13 around 1720, Kris Alageswaram (age unknown) was leading pitch number 26 on the Nose Route of El Capitan. At a height of 15 to 20 feet above the belay ledge, Kris placed a piece of protection for an aid move. While putting weight on the gear placement, the piece pulled out, and Kris fell about 15 to 20 feet hitting a sloping ledge with his leg. Kris continued to fall an additional 15 to 20 feet before the rope stopped his fall. His partner, David Reynolds, assisted Kris back to the belay ledge and they started yelling for help.

On September 14 Martin Ziebell was lowered approximately 800 feet to the injured climber. After stabilizing the open ankle fracture, he and the victim were raised to the summit. The victim was then carried approximately a quarter mile to a landing zone and flown to Crane Flat Heli-base to rendezvous with an air ambulance. The victim was then flown to Doctor's Medical Center in Modesto. Meanwhile, SAR team member Dean Potter was lowered to "Camp 5" to extract the victim's partner. Both were raised safely to the summit of El Capitan. All rescue personnel and equipment were then flown to CFH and transported by ground vehicle to the Valley SAR cache by 1800.

Analysis

Reynolds feels that the fall was caused by "bad gear placement."

Reynolds stated that he had been climbing for 15 years and that Kris had been climbing for 18 years. This was the fourth "Big Wall" in Yosemite that Reynolds and Alageswaram had climbed together. The other routes included "The Prow," and three years ago the two had climbed "The Regular Northwest Face of Half Dome" and "The South Face of Washington Column."

Reynolds indicated that Krishna was unhappy because he had a lot of weight on—including a large wall-rack. They did not have a hammer or pitons. He placed a small Alien camming device in a peg scar and stepped in his aider, and it ripped. He fell about 15 feet, hit a sloping ledge around the same level as my belay, and that's when his foot was turned and broken.

From the belay, Krishna had climbed up a little slab with mantle-shelf moves, face climbing with no way to protect it, no cracks. He tried to use the first possible gear placement, to aid the move, and that was the placement that didn't hold. He fell the 15 feet, hit the sloping ledge, and fell a further 15 feet, whereupon he came into Reynolds' belay and stopped.

Reynolds was pulled out of the ledge, but held his fall. He got him on a Jumar, tied him off, and rigged a system so he could haul him back onto the ledge. Krishna was able, using his good leg, to Jumar, while Reynolds held him on the Jumar and helped him onto the ledge. (Source: From reports by John Dill and Keith Lober, SAR Rangers, Yosemite National Park)

STRANDED, DARKNESS—FAILURE TO TURN BACK, INADEQUATE CLOTH-ING and EQUIPMENT
California, Yosemite Valley, Royal Arches

On September 15 at 2200, NPS dispatch received a report of climbers who were yelling for help on the Royal Arches Route. Rangers Keith Lober and John Dill and two SAR technicians responded on the call. Lighting systems, spotting scope and a loud hailer were utilized to identify the problem.

The two climbers, Andy Sneddon (35) and Debbie Hughes (35) were uninjured but had become disoriented in the darkness during the rappels. The team was unable to locate their stranded rappel anchor stations. This left them stranded near the ends of their ropes but still securely tied to anchors.

The climbers were left on the ledge for the night. No attempts were made to retrieve Sneddon and Hughes because the night was quite warm and they were not in danger of falling. Early the next morning, Ranger Keith Lober and SAR technician Werner Braun, risked their lives while they were climbing up to rescue Sneddon and Hughes. The two climbers were brought down without incident.

Analysis

This is the third of the Royal Arches descent incidents. Again, turning back earlier, having warm clothing, and knowing how to prusik came into play. (Source: Report from Keith Lober and John Dill, SAR Rangers, Yosemite National Park)

FALLING BAG OF ROCKS—HAUL ROPE SEVERED, POOR POSITION, INEXPERIENCE
California, Yosemite Valley, El Capitan

On October 8 at 1430, Daniel Gibson was practicing haul techniques by raising a 40 pound bag of rocks to his belay point. The bag became hung up on an overhang approximately 75 feet in the air. The rope failed, causing the bag of rocks to fall, hitting Helen Gibson (30) on the right side of her body, injuring her right arm and right leg. Rangers arrived on scene at 1440, immobilized, treated, and packaged Gibson. She was transported by litter reaching Medic 3 ambulance at 1558. (Source: Loren Fazio, Yosemite National Park)

Analysis

Apparently the rope abraded on a sharp edge on the overhang. Attention to where one is positioned relative to the fall line under such circumstances is a critical factor. Learning can be painful sometimes. (Source: Jed Williamson)

FALL ON ROCK, FATIGUE—UNABLE TO CLIP CARABINER
California, Pinnacles National Monument

The accident happened on September 25 at the Pinnacles Monument around noon. My climbing partner, Jamey Stowell, and I were on our fourth climb of the day, and climbing well. We were on "Cantaloupe Death" on the Monolith, a sport climb that has a trick start (5.10c) and then moves right around a slight bulge, easing into a more mellow (5.9) climb to the top. The climb itself starts not at the base of the rock, but rather from the top of a rock ledge about four feet across from the climb, about 10–12 feet above the ground. The belayer stands at ground level. To start the climb, you lean across this gap onto the face of the rock, grab some large holds, and jump onto the face and start climbing. Jamey led this climb first. When it came to my turn, I successfully struggled through the first move and was relieved that it was not as tough as I had anticipated. Now, I thought, I just had the more enjoyable section of the climb.

The next bolt for protection was up right toward the more mellow section of the climb, a point probably about 35 feet from the ground, and 20 feet from the ledge. My mind was relaxed, but I think that my hands were a bit tired from the first set of moves. When I got to the bolt, I had a difficult time finding a comfortable position from which to put the rope through the bolt. My right foothold was on a somewhat overhanging part of the rock, and my left hand was on a small knob, but I went to make the clip with my right hand anyway, confident that my hand would hold. When I went to make the clip, I found that the gate of the carabiner was pointing in the opposite direction than optimum, and after a couple of awkward attempts at making the clip, I decided to switch hands and clip with my left hand, repositioning my feet as well. This did not work either, and the possibility of falling flashed across my mind as I felt the strength in my hand draining. I think I had just pulled the rope up for slack to try and clip when I fell. The next thing I knew, I felt a "thud" on my tail end and left buttock, and my entire waist down a "zinging," a full body version of when one strikes the funny bone in the elbow. I had fallen about 20 feet and hit the ledge. As Jamey and I both remember, the rope began to stretch (and therefore absorb some of the fall) just as I hit the rock, so perhaps the fall was the equivalent of a 15-footer. Most definitely without an alert belayer, the fall and injury would have been considerably worse.

I bounced off the ledge, and Jamey lowered me the rest of the way down to the ground. I looked at my feet through the pain and was relieved to see that I could move them, albeit not very easily. Jamey summoned help from a nearby pair of climbers (who had, in fact, recommended Cantaloupe Death to us). They immediately came to our help. Jamey coiled up the rope to sling over his shoulders and piggy-backed me sitting in this sling about a mile and a half to the parking lot, where we were fortunate to find a pair of very helpful park employees who radioed for help. The park EMT arrived shortly, and we proceeded to make a decision about whether to call an ambulance or to drive on our own to the hospital in Hollister, about 40 miles away. We opted to stabilize my spine (a lovely experience being strapped onto a stiff board) and await paramedics, a decision that was well advised since the extent of spinal damage was unknown.

X-rays of my back at the hospital in Hollister showed a fractured coccyx, but no evidence of spinal damage. That allowed me to breathe a sigh of relief, and gave me the courage to call my wife to tell her that there had been a little accident.

The following Monday I went to my own HMO and the doctor there suspected that there might be something more than a broken tailbone going on because of continued pain in both of my feet. An MRI of my back showed indeed that I had sustained a fracture of the first lumbar (L1). The vertebra was compressed to about half its normal length (yes, I am now that much shorter), and the impact caused a contusion of the spinal cord, which explained my painful feet because the swelling puts pressure on the nerves. All of this will get better with time as the swelling subsides in three weeks or so. There is enough room in the spinal cavity for the recovery to be back to normal. But the vivid picture that remains is how close I had come—millimeters—to severely damaging my spinal cord at L1 which, as the neurologist pointed out, would have resulted in "wheelchair and loss of bowel control." Sobering words indeed. Again, I am thankful that Jamey was able to absorb some of the fall with his alert belaying!

Analysis

As for what I have learned about climbing safety, I offer the following observations. I think that the accident was a combination of mental and physical factors. As I think back, I had no fear on this climb, but that was because I had not calculated the ledge as a potential place where I might fall. My mind thought that I was about 35 feet above the ground, where indeed I was only 20 feet from the ledge. I certainly did not think I would hit the ground if I fell. Had I been aware of this danger, I might have avoided pushing off the face as I fell, or acted differently, maybe even be more determined not to fall. Had the climb been rated "R" (for "runout"), I might have paid attention to potential dangers, so I now know to approach any climb as a potential R or X. I also think that the "phew" factor of having made it through the first section of the climb was significant in letting down my guard. I was then surprised by how difficult the supposedly mellow section felt. If I had continued to be vigilant, I could have thought about alternative positions for clipping. In fact, I think that if I had gone up a little higher, my foot would have been in a less bulky section and I would have been in a better position. Had I been higher up with respect to the bolt, I would also not have had to pull up as much slack in the rope as I made my clip.

Another observation made by Jamey was the importance of wearing a helmet. That day, we had brought a helmet with us, but neither of us chose to wear it. If my foot position had been wrong when I fell, the rope could have flipped me over in mid air, and it is entirely possible that I could have landed on the ledge not on my behind, but on my head, a thought that makes me happy to have only a painful rear end!

Alternately, I could have fallen not on the ledge but in between the face and the ledge, and because that is a narrow space, I could have bounced around and hit my head on either wall. In any event, a helmet would have prevented serious head trauma. I have tended to think of helmets mostly as a precaution against falling rocks, but I now think that even in sport climbing, they are imperative—just as in bicycling. (Source: Kenji Hakuta)

FATIGUE, FALL ON ROCK, PROTECTION PULLED OUT
Colorado, Eldorado Canyon State Park

On January 17, a climber (male – 25) with limited experience and unfamiliar with "Dirt Deed" (5.6) the route he was on, became fatigued upon approaching the first ledge of the first pitch. His belayer observed him stopping to rest. As he continued to climb, he slipped and fell backwards. After about a 30-foot drop, one of the pieces of protection pulled, and he fell about another 50 feet hitting the rock wall several times. He ended hanging upside down and experienced massive trauma to the head, neck, and body. By the time he was lowered to the ground, fellow climbers noted that he had no pulse and was not breathing. He was not able to be resuscitated. (Source: Steve Muelhauser, Park Manager, and Conrad Bieniulis, Seasonal Park Ranger)

RAPPEL /LOWERING FAILURE—ROPE END PASSED THROUGH BELAY DEVICE
Colorado, Eldorado State Park

The route Washington Irving (5.6) is on the West Ridge and starts from a ledge 30 feet from the base of the rock that requires a fourth class scramble for access. On February 8, a belayer (female – 23) positioned herself on the ledge, thirty feet off the ground. She did not have a knot in her end of the rope, nor was it tied into her harness. Her partner (male 23) was an experienced climber, He had completed the first pitch of the climb, clipped the rope through fixed anchors, and was being lowered. As he descended towards the start of the climb on the ledge, the rope passed through the belay device and he fell past the ledge down the remaining 30 feet to the base, suffering a fracture in his left ankle and no other significant injuries. He was wearing a helmet at the time.

Analysis

Tying a knot in the end of the rope or tying the end to the harness can prevent this kind of incident. Climbing partners are advised to double check each other's gear before beginning. (Source: Steve Muelhauser, Park Manager, and Conrad Bieniulis, Seasonal Park Ranger)

FALLING ROCK, POOR POSITION
Colorado, Eldorado State Park

On February 22, a thirty year old female climber was walking along the base of the Rincon Wall when she was struck on the right forearm by a falling rock about the size of a climbing helmet. Her only warning came too late from a party of climbers directly above her. The rock had been dislodged by another party further above who failed to provide any verbal warning. The victim sustained some bruises and was assisted by her climbing partner and a nurse who was climbing nearby.

Analysis

In heavily trafficked areas especially, climbers must provide immediate and clearly audible warning to anyone in the surrounding area if they dislodge a rock. Conversely, climbers should consider their position beneath another climbing party—unless they knowingly assume the associated risks. Hikers in a climbing area should also be on the alert for falling objects and avoid walking directly beneath climbing routes. A helmet is certainly a good idea when in a place where falling rocks and/or objects are a possibility. (Source: Steve Muelhauser, Park Manager, and Conrad Bieniulis, Seasonal Park Ranger)

FALL ON ICE, INADEQUATE KNOT
Colorado, Ouray Ice Park

On March 19, Greg Kowalsky (age unknown) fell 70 feet when his knot came undone as he was preparing to be lowered by his partner who was belaying him from the ground.

Despite efforts of emergency crews and four nearby climbers, Kowalsky succumbed to his multiple injuries. (Source: *The Ridgeway Sun*, Week of March 19–25, 1998)

(Editor's Note: This park was featured on the cover of last year's ANAM journal. Though this was the first fatality in the four years of operation of the facility, many stories of "near misses" involving similar problems are passing down the grapevine. It's a place where many individuals are trying ice climbing for the first time.)

FALL ON ROCK, DESCENDING UNROPED, NO HELMET
Colorado, Eldorado State Park

On March 25, a thirty-two year old female experienced climber and her partner had just completed the first pitch of Blind Faith (5.10) on the west side of the Bastille. Rather than continuing up the route or rigging a rappel, they decided to unrope and down-climb a somewhat loose, broken cleft in the cliff. During the down-climb the victim fell, falling about 50 feet to the ground. She was not tied into a rope and had no helmet on at the time. She suffered multiple lacerations to her forehead, right hand, and right ankle as well as a loss of sensation below her waist. She was later diagnosed to have fractured her spine and damaged her spinal cord. (Source: Steve Muelhauser, Park Manager, and Conrad Bieniulis, Seasonal Park Ranger)

FALL ON ROCK
Colorado, Eldorado Canyon State Park

On June 7, a thirty-nine-year-old male experienced climber had started to follow the fourth pitch of Ruper (5.8) on Redgarden Wall when he reached for a hand hold, missed and fell. The belayer cinched the rope, but since his follower had just started the pitch, there was sufficient stretch to allow the victim to contact a ledge with enough impact to rip his shoe off his left foot. He suffered a severe sprain to his left foot but was able to rappel down to the base of the climb and left the park with only minor assistance from rescue personnel. He stated that a hole in the sole of his shoe contributed to his accident. He did have a helmet on at the time. (Source: Steve Muelhauser, Park Manager.)

STRANDED—FATIGUE, INEXPERIENCE, MISCOMMUNICATION
Colorado, Eldorado State Park

On June 13, a twenty-one-year-old male with moderate climbing experience was seconding the second pitch of the Bulge (5.7) at Redgarden Wall when he fell about three feet. After a brief rest, he attempted the move repeatedly and failed each time. By this time, the victim was tiring and due to high wind conditions and lack of a line of sight to his belayer was unable to communicate his dilemma to the belayer above. The victim clipped into a fixed piece of hardware and did not move. He was approximately 150 feet above the ground at this point. After about half an hour of waiting, the belayer decided to tie off his rope and soloed off the route to get help, but did not inform the victim. Rescue personnel finally contacted the victim, set up an anchor above and rappelled down to him. They were able to rappel him and his gear to safety. He was not injured. Neither he nor the belayer had a helmet on during the climb.

Analysis

Conditions of high winds and restricted visibility require extra measures of precaution and a backup system of communication such as a rope tug code between partners. Climbers should not exceed their abilities, particularly if the partners are not familiar with each other's experience and skill level. (Source: Steve Muelhauser, Park Manager, and Conrad Bieniulis, Seasonal Park Ranger)

FALL ON ROCK—UNABLE TO SELF-RESCUE
Colorado, Eldorado State Park

On August 8, A twenty-eight-year-old male experienced climber was leading the fourth pitch of Rewritten (5.7) on Redgarden Wall when he slipped and fell twelve feet. The victim's protection held and the belayer was able to stop the fall. However, the victim's lower right leg caught on a rock during the incident resulting in a multiple fracture to that leg. Because of their location on the route approximately 300 feet above the ground, the belayer was unable to lower the victim down. A nearby climber witnessed the fall and called 911 on his cellular phone. Rescue personnel reached the victim from the base of Rewritten. They stabilized his leg and lowered him to safety. (Source: Steve Muelhauser, Park Ranger)

RAPPEL ERROR—ROPES UNEVEN, RAPPEL OFF END OF ROPE, NO HELMET
Colorado, Eldorado State Park

Just Another Girl's Climb (5.12) on Lower Peanuts Wall begins on a ledge about fifty feet off the ground requiring a scramble for access. On September 6, a forty-two year old male experienced climber had lowered his partner who unsuccessfully attempted a lead on this route back down to the ledge. The victim then decided to scramble to the top of the route and rappel down. The victim ran his rope through the fixed anchor and successfully rappelled for the first forty to fifty feet until he rappelled off one end of the rope. The victim then fell about twenty to thirty feet down to the ledge where his partner was still positioned. The victim fell to the ledge and continued falling the additional fifty feet to the ground. The victim did not check to see if the ends were even nor did he tie knots in the ends of the rope prior to rappelling. He was not wearing a helmet. The victim suffered multiple abrasions and lacerations over his body as well as severe fractures to his shoulder and left leg. (Source: Steve Muelhauser, Park Manager, and Conrad Bieniulis, Seasonal Park Ranger)

(Editor's Note: Reports from Eldorado Canyon and a few other locations in Colorado were received for 1997 following publication of last year's ANAM. They have been put into the data. Among these incidents, of which there were eight, were two fatalities, one caused as a result of not wearing a helmet, and the other due to an ice climber not being anchored. Five of the incidents involved injuries that could have been prevented by wearing a helmet. One serious injury resulted when a belayer was using a figure of eight for a device in the same manner as it is used for a rappel. The friction was inadequate, and the rope passed through the device, causing the climber to drop to the ground. Another fall was the result of an experienced climber tying in only to the elastic part of his harness. He survived a long fall, but suffered serious head injury and seizures.)

FALL ON ROCK, INADEQUATE (NO) BELAY, MISCOMMUNICATION
Colorado, Rocky Mountain National Park, Lumpy Ridge

On August 9, Stewart Ritchie (38) fell 60 feet from the top of the route Ziggie's Day Out (I, 5.10b) on Checkerboard Rock at Lumpy Ridge. Ritchie had completed his lead of the route, and clipped a second rope that he had been trailing through the top anchors. Ritchie's plan was to be lowered off the route via this second rope. However, there was miscommunication between Ritchie and his belayer, Steve Britt. Britt did not place Ritchie on belay on the second rope, and Britt had also removed the belay from the lead rope. Subsequently, when Ritchie leaned back to be lowered off the cliff, he fell unbelted from either line. Ritchie's ground fall resulted in fractured leg, abrasions, and possible internal injuries.

Analysis

The members of this team were international level climbers with guiding experience. They had a casual attitude and approach to enjoying this short, fun route. Assumptions about what his partner was doing led Ritchie to this unfortunate result. (Source: Jim Detterline, RMNP Ranger)

STRANDED, PARTY SEPARATED, FAILED TO FOLLOW ROUTE, EXCEEDING ABILITIES
Colorado, Rocky Mountain National Park, Notchtop

On August 21, Wes Oren (age unknown) had completed an ascent of the Spiral Route (III, 5.4) on Notchtop with two companions. At 2030, Oren separated from his companions while searching for the proper descent, a fourth class gully. Oren ended up stranded on a cliff band just below the North Face. He sustained minor abrasions and inflamed a pre-existing injury to his left wrist. Oren became benighted on the cliff band. He was rescued by rangers at 0633 on the following morning.

Analysis

The textbook *Mountaineering: Freedom of the Hills* contains an excellent section on group dynamics which states that the leader is responsible for the safety and success of the climb or outing. In this case, the leader had difficulty finding the descent and then allowed an inexperienced climber to separate from and lose sight of the rest of the party. Instead of finding their missing companion, the two partners left the scene and reported it to rangers to complete what became an overnight search and rescue. To Oren's credit, he had enough survival savvy to survive an uncomfortable night out. (Source: Jim Detterline, RMNP Ranger)

FALL ON ROCK, PARTY SEPARATED, EXCEEDING ABILITIES
Colorado, Quandry Mountain

On September 6, two climbers, a woman named Sunny (40) and her companion, a man (42), were ascending the Class 4 West Ridge on Quandry Mountain when Sunny slipped on loose rock and fell 300 feet down a couloir. The victim was attended to by nearby medical personnel. SAR personnel arrived with a paramedic. The victim was removed by helicopter to hospital, but expired the next morning.

Analysis

The victim's companion said that she had hiked very quickly ahead of him, around a gendarme. He heard a cry, then saw her cartwheel down the couloir. (Source: Summit County Rescue Group)

FALL ON SNOW, UNABLE TO SELF-ARREST, INADEQUATE PROTECTION, EXCEEDING ABILITIES
Colorado, Rocky Mountain National Park, Long's Peak

On September 19, at 0930, Mike Riter (23) and partner Simeon Bateman (24) were ascending Lamb's Slide on the east face of Long's Peak with intentions of doing the Kiener's Route to the summit. Both men were wearing crampons and using single mountaineering axes. They were roped together and were "simul-climbing" but without intermediate protection. Bateman, about one third of the way up Lamb's Slide and in the lead, slipped on the hard-packed icy snow and failed to self-arrest. Bateman slid past Riter and pulled Riter with him. Riter was dragged for 100 feet or more and was then able to self-arrest. Bateman slid nearly 300 feet and was stopped by Riter's self-arrest only 50 feet above the rocks at the edge of Mills Glacier. Bateman sustained a deep puncture wound to his right calf from being impaled by his own Black Diamond scissors style crampons. Riter injured both elbows and his right ankle.

Analysis

Bateman and Riter were both professional outdoor equipment salesmen, who had about five years' climbing experience on rock. However, both were relatively inexperienced at snow and ice climbing. Bateman and Riter had climbed Kiener's Route during Summer 1997, but snow conditions were friendlier at that time. An alternative strategy to climb Lamb's Slide when either conditions or inexperience make self-arrest ineffective is to climb next to the rock wall on the right, either belaying protected pitches or "simul-climbing." "Simul-climbing" is only truly executed when there are at least two or three points of protection at all times on the rope between the climbers. Lamb's Slide has been the scene of various disasters, reenactments of Rev. Elkanah Lamb's 1871 slide of about 1,000 feet. (Source: Jim Detterline, RMNP Ranger)

FALL ON ICE, CLIMBING ALONE, INADEQUATE PROTECTION
Colorado, Rocky Mountain National Park, Thatchtop

On November 15, at 1000, Richard Ladue (37) was doing an unroped solo of All Mixed Up (III, WI4) on Thatchtop when he fell 100 feet to the base of the route. Two nearby ice climbers witnessed the accident, but were unsure if the fall was due to brittle, broken ice or to faulty technique. Ladue sustained a depressed skull fracture on his left temple, below the rim of his helmet, and other lesser injuries. Ladue died in the litter of complications due to the head injury at 1900, 500 feet from the base of the route, as the park's rescuers were working on his evacuation.

Analysis

The risks and consequences of unroped solo climbing are multiplied when the medium is ice, considering the changeable and inconsistent nature of ice. To make solo climbing safer, a self-belayed rope system may be employed. Also, the solo is often safer if the route chosen is several levels below the climber's ability. Ladue wore a helmet, and it is most unfortunate that he was struck below the protection of the helmet. Ladue was an experienced ice climber who had previously climbed All Mixed Up.

The conditions of ice on All Mixed Up were on the thin side due to wind driven sublimation and intense climbing by numerous parties. The route would have been a safer choice in fatter conditions, but as the ice conditions improve, generally the avalanche hazard from a bowl atop the climb increases. (Source: Jim Detterline, RMNP Ranger)

FALL ON ROCK—FOOT HOLD BROKE OFF, PROTECTION PULLED
Idaho, Sawtooth Wilderness, Grandjean Peak

On August 29, Mick Riffie and myself (we are both from Boise, Idaho) were attempting a new route on the Northeast Face of Grandjean Peak in the

Sawtooth Wilderness in Idaho. The route consisted of about 2000 feet of very moderate climbing on granite (about 1000 feet of 5.3–5.4 slabs, 500 feet of 5.7 chimneys and slabs and the remainder assorted scrambling). We were about 1200 feet into the climb and I was leading the start of a two pitch 5.7 section. I was just past the halfway point on the first pitch, and a nubbin I was standing on broke out from under my foot. I was about 15 feet above my last piece of protection (a #1 tri-cam set in the cam position). I fell onto the cam and felt the rope come tight, then watched the cam fly very forcefully out of the rock. I fell another ten feet and hit a small ledge, which knocked me backwards, causing me to hit my head, and continue a tumbling fall to the next piece of pro about 20 feet farther down. The total fall distance was approximately 70 feet.

The blow to my head was forceful enough to crack my helmet, and I sustained many injuries (severe concussion, broken nose, sprained wrist, sprained knee, many deep bruises and abrasions, and multiple facial and leg lacerations). I was unable to walk, and my partner rappelled and down climbed to get help which was approximately six hours one way.

Analysis

The rock in the area is granite, and the quality of the rock changes from very solid to somewhat crumbly and questionable throughout the route. My experience is ten years of mixed rock and alpine mountaineering. This year I had successfully climbed many 5.8–5.9 routes in the Sawtooths and had also climbed Mount Rainier via Liberty Ridge, and Mount Robson via the Kain Face earlier in the summer. I felt very comfortable in the route we were on at the time. I also believe that my helmet saved my life, and have always been a strong advocate of wearing one. (Source: Greg Parker)

AVALANCHE
Nevada, Spring Mountain Ranch, Kyle Canyon

On March 24, Russ Peterson (40) an Las Vegas Metropolitan Police Dept. SAR Officer, and J. R., LVMPD SAR Volunteer, snow shoed in to Angel Falls in Kyle Canyon to climb the Hosemonster (WI5). Snowfall had been heavy that winter and Angel Falls had frozen wide and thick on its 80-foot lower section. The upper 200-foot section was wide and thick at the base but tapered to three feet at it's top. A steep snow slope met the base of the route with a foot wide moat separating the snow from the ice.

Peterson led the first section of ice to the large alcove below the upper section. He called down that the upper tier of ice looked solid and climbable, but that the snow in the alcove was loose and unconsolidated. They decided to take turns top-roping the lower section. Peterson established an anchor with several equalized screws and pound-ins and lowered to the base.

His partner climbed the lower pitch, removing the screws Peterson had placed on lead. At the anchor, he heard a loud crack and rumbling and called "Avalanche!" He pulled close to the ice and felt it wash over him. When it stopped, he looked down and saw that Peterson was partially buried by the ice and not moving. Looking up, he saw that the top 100 feet of the upper tier of the Hosemonster had broken free. Peterson had kept him on belay and the rope was now taut through the anchor to his harness. He made a "z-rig" using prusiks and a cordalette to get enough slack in the rope to untie. Before he could free himself, he again heard a loud crack and rumble as the bottom half of the upper section broke free and washed over him. Peterson was now completely buried. J. R. was able to untie and secure the rope to the anchor and descend using prusiks and the cordalette about an hour after the initial ice fall.

Peterson never moved following the initial ice fall and was found apneic and pulseless. His partner snow-shoed out and radioed for help on reaching the truck. Peterson's body was recovered by LVMPD Officers and Volunteers the next morning.

Analysis

The top of the upper section of the Hosemonster is often poorly bonded to the rock. It is likely that the upper section broke free of its own weight. Wearing a helmet is vital. Peterson died instantly under the tons of ice that fell from above. His helmet offered no protection. His partner was partially sheltered and his helmet proved lifesaving. Peterson had built a solid multi-point equalized anchor that held despite taking impact from the falling ice. He also kept his partner on belay even in death. Self rescue skills, prusiks, and a cordalette for such an event, and being able to safely escape the anchor and descend to the snow allowed his partner to survive a catastrophic ice fall and walk out with minor contusions.

Russ Paterson was an exceptional man with a passion for climbing. He had recently begun climbing ice and that day had affirmed his passion for it. Russ is deeply missed by his team members and fellow officers, and we will never fill the void left by his passing. (Source: James Roberts, Volunteer, Las Vegas Metropolitan Police Department SAR)

STRANDED—EXCEEDING ABILITIES, INADEQUATE CLOTHING
Nevada, Red Rock Canyon National Conservation Area, Juniper Canyon

On April 12, S. L., A. M., G. W. and C. J., all visiting from Canada, set off to climb Black Dagger (III, 5.7) in Juniper Canyon. The party had come to Red Rock intending to climb this route. Darkness found them stuck on a ledge, possibly off route, with temperatures near freezing and winds gusting to 40 mph. At 2130, S.L. called 911 by cellular phone. The Las Vegas Metropolitan Police Department's SAR coordinator Sgt. Clint Bassett, was notified. S.L. explained that the party was about one pitch from the top of the route, but wearing only shorts and T-shirts, and that they felt they would be unable to "make the night."

Officers and Volunteers of Metro's Search and Rescue unit met and staged at Pine Creek and LVMPD's Air 3, an MD 530F, entered Juniper Canyon to assess the scene. The crew of Air 3 located the party, but determined that inserting rescuers above the climbers would not be possible because of dangerous turbulence and high winds.

An overland approach from Lovell Canyon to the west of the Red Rock escarpment was decided upon, and at 0230 one officer and nine LVMPD SAR volunteers left from the Bridge Mount. Trailhead. After several hours of hiking over rough terrain, the team came within a mile of the top of Juniper Canyon. It was determined that significant technical operations would be needed to access the top of the cliff and would be unsafe due to darkness, high winds, cold and rescuer fatigue. At about 0600, this team turned back.

At 0700, Air 3 reentered the canyon and again found winds and turbulence too severe to safely insert a team from above. A second LVMPD team of one officer and four volunteers began briefing to access the climber's via the walk off for Black Dagger. This team departed at 0830.

At the same time the 66th Air Rescue Squadron from Nellis Air Force Base was contacted about using their aircraft to effect the rescue. At 0920, an MH-60 Pave Hawk, call sign 007, arrived and at 0930 was able to locate the climbers with direction from Air 3. At 0945, two PJ's were lowered to the victims who had finished the remaining 300 feet of slabs to the top the Black Dagger. At 1045, after 007 returned from burning off excess fuel, the climbers were hoisted out in pairs and returned to the Pine Creek CP. The two LVMPD teams returned to the CP.

The four climbers were all still shivering, but were uninjured. None were in T-shirts as had been claimed, only one was in shorts, and all had some outer wear.

Analysis
S.L. stated that they had talked to other climbers and BLM rangers regarding the route, and had called the Weather Service and received a forecast of light winds. Despite this, S.L. felt they had underestimated the approach and the route, and were several hours behind their established schedule when darkness fell. Three of the party had more that three years of climbing experience, one had only one year, and S.L. felt that the last climber's inexperience had slowed them down.

Balmy spring days typically turn into very cold nights at Red Rock. Many routes in the canyons require two hours for the approach, and just as much time for the descent. Climbing these routes can be an all day affair, and when darkness falls, route finding is difficult and steep brushy walk off's can be deadly. This party did well to stop and huddle together to keep warm rather than continue in darkness and risk injury or separation. Having a cellular phone to call for help was also prudent. This also demonstrates that the ability to call 911 is no guarantee of a timely rescue or surviving the night exposed to freezing temperatures. Another consideration is that the rescue was carried out based on the claim that the party was under clothed and unlikely to "make the night." It is never appropriate to embellish your situation's severity to avoid an uncomfortable night in the cold. For all intents and purposes, this party was able to self rescue from the route, and likely could have done the walk off in daylight unaided—without, thereby, unfairly jeopardizing the lives of the 30 rescuers who responded to their call. (Source: James Roberts, Volunteer, Las Vegas Metropolitan Police Department SAR)

FALL ON ROCK—HAND-HOLD BROKE OFF
Nevada, Red Rock National Conservation Area, Magic Bus

About noon on April 18, L.C., an experienced local climber (25), was leading Blonde Dwarf (5.10) on the Magic Bus, in the Red Rock Canyon National Conservation Area. He was 15 to 20 feet above his last protection and very close to the final anchors when a hand hold broke. According to his partners, L. C. fell about 30 feet before being caught by the rope. He was lowered to the base of the route by his partners.

Officers and volunteers of the Las Vegas Metropolitan Police Department's Search and Rescue unit were conducting helicopter training at the top of the Red Rock escarpment at the time. At 1220, they were notified of the incident and a team of one officer and nine volunteers was shuttled to the accident site by Air 5, an HH-1H. Air 5 was able to insert the team by skid down hover about 100 feet from the victim.

L. C. was assessed to have superficial abrasions and contusions from the fall, but was complaining of lumbar back pain and numbness and tingling in his legs. He was unable to move his legs. L. C. was immobilized, packaged in a litter and at 1306 was lowered to the LZ using a low angle system. At 1315, Air 5 again performed a skid down hover, the victim and mission medic were loaded and flown to the CP. At 1320, the victim was handed over to Valley Hospital's Flight for Life and flown to University Medical Center's Trauma Center. By 1430, all personnel had been recovered from the rescue and training sites.

Analysis

When the hold broke, L. C. fell backward, and was horizontal when his harness caught him. Despite a successful belay, and the lack of a hard impact, L. C.'s spine was damaged and he is paralyzed. It is rare for sport climbers to wear helmets and in this instance it was not an issue. While a full strength chest harness may have caused a more upright catch and affected the outcome, countless similar falls are taken every year without injury. (Source: James Roberts, Volunteer, Las Vegas Metropolitan Police Department SAR)

FALL ON ROCK, INADEQUATE PROTECTION, NO HARD HAT
Nevada, Red Rocks Canyon National Conservation Area, Lost Creek

On December 5, C. A. and a friend, both visiting from Austria, were climbing in the Lost Creek area of the Red Rock Canyon Conservation Area. At 1640 C. A. (19) began climbing in a corner to the right of Little Big Horn. C. A., who was not wearing a helmet, had climbed 30 feet up without placing any protection when he slipped and fell backwards to the ground, striking his head.

C. A.'s partner called for help, and hikers in the area contacted Las Vegas Metropolitan Police dispatch. LVMPD Officers and Volunteers responded and well as a Las Vegas Fire Department paramedic engine.

On their arrival, three firefighters with advanced life support equipment hiked 20 minutes to the victim and began care. LVMPD SAR officers and volunteers arrived shortly after. The victim's location above a slope of dense scrub oak, manzanita and large boulders made a carry out or conventional helicopter evacuation impossible, so it was decided to short haul him to the trailhead.

C. A. was unresponsive and posturing and LVFD paramedics were unable to intubate him. C. A. was immobilized on a Miller board by SAR personnel, placed in a litter and carried 50 yards to an open area where he was short hauled with an LVMPD SAR Officer to the trailhead by Air 4, an MD530F. C. A. was transferred to the waiting Flight for Life helicopter crew who intubated C. A. en route to UMC Trauma Center. C. A. died several days later of isolated head injuries. (Source: James Roberts, Volunteer, Las Vegas Metropolitan Police Department SAR)

STRANDED, EXCEEDING ABILITIES, INADEQUATE CLOTHING, DARKNESS, WEATHER
Nevada, Red Rock Canyon National Conservation Area, White Rock Springs
Late on the morning of December 21, T. W. (13) and J. P. (18) began climbing Tunnel Vision (III, 5.7) on the Angel Food Wall. Darkness found them at the bottom of the fifth pitch in the mouth of the "tunnel."

T. W.'s parents became concerned when he did not return home and called BLM Rangers about 1800. They found J. P.'s car in the White Rock Spring parking area. Ranger Chuck Ward advised LVMPD SAR Coordinator Sgt. Basset. A LVMPD SAR officer and volunteer met J. P.'s father and BLM Rangers at the victim's car with the intention of walking half a mile to the base of the route and checking the walk-off for the victims. J. P.'s father advised that the climbers were wearing light fleece tops with no shell gear, had no lights or helmets. Air temperature was in the thirties, winds were 10–20 mph and it was snowing.

At 2030, during a lull in the wind, rescuers called out for the victims over a vehicle PA. Much to their surprise, the victims called back, shouting their location, that they were OK, and did not need to be rescued "unless it gets colder or wet." It began snowing harder, winds increased and voice contact was no longer possible. Sgt. Basset arrived on scene, and after discussing the options, it was decided to page out the team's Volunteers, discuss insertion options with the LVMPD rescue pilots and get a weather forecast from the FAA. By 2100 14 Volunteers had arrived as had another LVMPD SAR Officer who had brought the helicopter fuel trailer. Because of the victim's ages, their lack of preparation and worsening weather, a rescue was begun.

Winds were gusting to 40 mph with light snow eliminating the possibility of a helicopter insertion that night. The forecast was for increased winds with gusts to 60 mph until 0400 when winds would decrease to 30–40 mph with temperatures in the upper 30s the next day. It was decided to send a team up the walk-off to raise the victims after first light. A team of ten Volunteers and one Officer left the parking lot at 2300 with clearing skies, cold temperatures and high winds. Snow on the ground made finding the trail to the base impossible, so the team hiked cross country to the base of the walk off. The walk-off is a steep boulder and brush choked gully. The team, with technical rescue gear, negotiated 600 feet of fourth and fifth class terrain, arriving on a ledge system near the top of Tunnel Vision about 0520. The sky had cleared and winds were still blowing at 40 mph across the cliffs.

At sunrise winds diminished unexpectedly. The team moved above the route and with the use of a spotting scope from the trailhead were guided onto a rock outcrop above the tunnel's exit. Anchors and lowering systems were established and a SAR Volunteer was lowered 300 feet through the tunnel's exit. On reaching the victims, he found that they were cold but uninjured. A hauling was established, and the team began raising the Volunteer and J. P. at 0950. Radio contact was intermittent and the belay line became snagged on the featured rock face above the tunnel. A second Volunteer rappelled to the snagged belay line, freed it at 1105 and the raise continued. The small working area and chicken-heads on the outcrop made the raise slow and strenuous for the haul team. At 1145, J. P. and rescuer were recovered at the haul ledge.

LVMPD Air 3, an MD530F, had flown a reconnaissance of the route and found that T. W., still in the mouth of the tunnel, could be reached by hoist. LVMPD Air 5, an HH-1H, responded, and at 1215 a SAR Volunteer was lowered by hoist in gusty conditions to the mouth of the tunnel. T. W. and rescuer were recovered at 1222, and Air 5 returned to the CP. The rescue systems were broken down and the team moved to a small LZ where they were extracted by Air 3 via one skid hover. The rescue was terminated at 1400.

Analysis

J. P. and T. W. are accomplished gym climbers, with apparently little outdoor experience. While Tunnel Vision can be done in five pitches, it is a long route to undertake on the shortest day of the year. Combined with a late start and inadequate clothing, they underestimated the route and conditions. They spent a cold night in the shelter of the tunnel and by morning, both had no feeling below their knees. Had they been stranded anywhere else on the route, both would likely have died. (Source: James Roberts, Volunteer – Las Vegas Metropolitan Police Department SAR)

FALLING ROCK
New Hampshire, Cannon Cliff, Sam's Swan Song

On May 17, John Bouchard and Mark Richey were climbing fast in preparation for an attempt on the Himalayan peak Latok. High on the cliff, Mark was climbing second to John when a large flake Mark had his arm behind detached from the cliff. Mark's arm was broken as the flake, described by two other climbers as the size of the bed of a pickup truck, slid off its ledge. The flake destroyed two lower ledges on Sam's on its way to the talus. John and Mark finished the climb and walked out on their own.

Analysis

Cannon is a cliff that has many very loose rocks—ranging from pebble to bus size—precariously perched everywhere. It is recommended that each and every hold be carefully analyzed and tested before using. With many years of climbing experience on this cliff, John and Mark were pushing the limits of speed during this training climb. It is possible that Mark's assessment of the flake was compromised by his desire to move fast; however, it should also be recognized that it is impossible to identify all loose rocks. Climbers should treat all holds as suspect. (Source: John Bouchard)

FALL ON ROCK, INADEQUATE PROTECTION—RAPPEL ANCHOR (PITONS) CAME OUT
New Hampshire, Cannon Cliff

On December 16, Tom Douglas (26) and I (29) hiked up to the base of Cannon Cliff to climb Black Dike, a moderate four-pitch mixed rock and ice climb. Finding a line of climbers waiting for the Dike, we decided instead to climb a harder line just to the right, called Fafnir. While following the final pitch (almost completely rock in the current conditions), Tom released an engine-sized block with his feet and watched it crash 300 feet to the ground. Thankfully, no one was hurt and we completed the three-pitch climb successfully without further incident about 1 p.m.

Hoping to have time to climb the Black Dike, we immediately began our rappel, using a single 60 meter rope and the fixed gear at the belay stations as anchors. Rappelling first, Tom neared the final anchor and realized that the rope did not quite reach the fixed gear (since the length of the rope allowed us to skip the second-to-last anchor). Tom told me that the rope did not reach and that he would down climb the remaining ten feet on moderate ice to the anchor. He clipped into the anchor and I rappelled to the end of the rope. I untied from the rope, passed him an end and then he threaded the rope through the fixed gear (two pitons connected with two slings) and began his rappel as I down climbed to the anchor to clip in. Just as he started rappelling, the anchors pulled out and he fell approximately 100–120 feet to the ground, bouncing twice on the way down and then rolling for about 20 feet on the 30-degree scree slope below. Tom stood up after about ten seconds and said that he had broken his right arm but was otherwise OK. It took me about fifteen minutes to down climb the last pitch, during which time Tom began walking down. I joined Tom and he completed the two-hour walk under his own power. At the hospital, we found that he had broken his left tibia, left hand, and a number of bones in his right arm.

Analysis

Lessons learned: always, always, check fixed gear and back up anything that looks even remotely unsafe. Also, it's easy to focus on the difficulties of the ascent of a climb and let your guard down during the descent. A climb is not over until you're safely at your car! (Source: Hank Midgley)

FALL ON ICE, INADEQUATE PROTECTION
New Hampshire, Mount Washington, Huntington Ravine, O'Dell's Gully

December 29, Greg Farrell (39) and Brian Carlock, both experienced ice climbers, were ascending O'Dell's Gully at 0815 in preparation for a trip to Mount Katahdin. Part of their training was to climb Pinnacle and O'Dell's in a day and employ the technique of "simul-climbing" to climb quicker on the easier sections. Neither of them had used this technique before.

Using a doubled 8.6 mm rope, they had at least one ice screw between them. The terrain was water ice, moderate angle. Brian was leading. With one screw in the ice, Greg stopped at the screw to wait for Brian to place a second ice screw before he removed the one he was at. Catching his crampon point on his bootstrap, Greg lost his balance and fell, pulling Brian with him. Sliding and bouncing down the ice, the single ice screw did hold their fall (the 17 cm, Yates Screamer had activated). Greg fell 13 meters while Brian fell 39 meters, and both ended up hanging side by side on the ice. Both seemed to be OK at this point, so Greg built an anchor where they were and lowered Brian down to the snow slope using an extra rope he had in his pack. Once at the base of the ice, Brain realized pain in his right hip would prevent him from standing, so a second climbing party used an ice anchor to lower Brian down the snow slope to the trail. Many nearby climbers assisted in getting Brian to the trail where he was carried out by litter. Later that evening, Brian was treated for his soft tissue injuries and released from the Androscoggin Medical Center.

Analysis

While simul-climbing is a technique used for moving quickly over moderate terrain, it is also dangerous because a slip by the second could easily pull the leader off, as happened in this accident. We should have had more protection between us. This technique calls for abundant protection even on easy terrain as these points are the only "belay" for the climbers, at least two points of pro between climbers. Because the terrain was easy, I was more "relaxed" and didn't have my axes planted well—they were dangling at my side—at the stance before the fall, which would've resulted in a stumble only. The leader should have his tools planted well and anchored to them while placing a screw, thus creating a temporary anchor for himself and partner. Even on easy terrain it is important to be constantly vigilant and to immediately have tools planted securely at stances, as portable belays. (Source: Greg Farrell)

(Editors Note: Jeff Fongemie points out the following. "Easy ice is not always about the angle of the ice. The ice on Mount. Washington is often very brittle and even low angle ice can be difficult. If, at a Mountain Rescue Service meeting here in North Conway, you asked how many have taken falls on low angle ice, you might be surprised to see how many highly experienced mountaineers raise their hands.")

FALL ON ICE, INADEQUATE PROTECTION
New Hampshire, Crawford Notch, Frankenstein Cliffs

On December 30 Bob O'Brien paired up with Lisa Thompson for some ice climbing. Bob is an experienced ice climber of more than ten years and while Lisa has limited experience with ice climbing, she has many years of rock climbing experience. They had not climbed together before.

Bob set off for a lead of Cave Route (NEI 3) with Lisa as the belayer. Cave Route is a one pitch route that begins with a 30 foot section of 55 to 60 degree ice followed by some vertical columns that are avoided by climbing around them on the left. Bob climbed to the top of the first section and placed an ice screw. Looking for a greater challenge, he headed up the 15-foot tall columns direct. Deciding the ice was too candled and poor in quality, he choose not to "waste time" attempting to place an ice screw, but instead climb to the top of the column and finish the climb. With his tools over the top of the column but feet still on the steep ice, his right tool came out of the ice, then his left tool also came out. Acting quickly, Bob was able to replace his left tool. Any feelings of safety melted as he "barn-doored" to the left and his left hand came out of the leash. With the tool remaining in the ice, he fell, pulling out his only ice screw along the way. Bob fell 40 feet to the ground. Nearby climbers, including a doctor and a paramedic, assisted in the half mile carry out using a litter from a rescue cache at the parking lot. Bob broke both his tibia and fibula of his left leg when his left foot caught the lower angle ice at the base of the column.

Analysis

The main problem here is of the climber not placing adequate protection. Once on the column, Bob had three alternatives. First, stop and take the time to place good protection. Second, conclude that he could not (for any reason) place the protection and retreat. Or third, conclude that he could not (for any reason) place the protection, keep climbing and risk ground fall, hoping that he would not fall. Bob chose the third alternative, but fell. As ice climbers, we sometimes do not place protection as frequently as we do on rock in the summer relying on hopefully solid ice tool placements. The merits of this can be argued both ways. Nevertheless, placing protection infrequently enough so that ground-fall is a possibility is never a good option, as we cannot be certain that we will not fall. (Source: Bob O'Brian and Lisa Thompson)

FAULTY USE OF CRAMPONS and LOSS OF CONTROL—VOLUNTARY GLISSADE, INADEQUATE EQUIPMENT—NO ICE AX
New Hampshire, Mount Washington, Tuckerman Ravine Trail

On December 30 there were two separate accidents involving sliding with crampons. In the first incident, a party of two was descending the Summit Cone by glissading with crampons on their feet. One of the climbers snagged his crampon and broke his ankle. Other climbers on the scene aided his continued descent down the Lions Head trail. In the second accident, a party of two climbing the summit cone had crampons on their feet and no ice axes. One tripped and with no ax to self arrest with, slid 300 feet into a rock outcrop badly dislocating his ankle in the process. Local Mountain Rescue Service member Brad White was nearby and assisted in the rescue using his ax as a splint. With a litter from the Mount. Washington Observatory on the summit, he was carried down Lion Head Trail.

Analysis

Snowstorms this winter had been ending as wet snow or rain followed by cold air. This makes for very icy conditions on Mount. Washington. The first incident is an example of why a climber should not glissade with crampons on. Having an ice ax in hand and knowing how to self-arrest with it could have prevented the second accident. (Source: Brad White, Mountain Rescue Service)

VARIOUS FALLS ON ROCK, RAPPEL/LOWERING FAILURES, AND INADEQUATE PROTECTION (INCLUDING NO HELMET)
New York, Mohonk Preserve, Shawangunks

There were 18 incidents reported from this popular climbing area this year. Of the twelve falls, six were the result of rappel or lowering errors. In four instances, protection came out and in another, no protection was put in, so the consequences of the fall were guaranteed. The average age of the climbers was 34, and the average degree of difficulty on which the climbing incidents occurred was between 5.7 and 5.8. We do not receive the level of experience information from this area, but some of the reports come in from the individuals involved or from someone who witnessed the scene.

There were some interesting causes in the "other" category. There was an individual who fell 20 feet after taking his harness off in an effort to try to get his rope unstuck. He walked away uninjured. In three cases, climbers fell when being lowered because the end of the rope went through the belay device, and in one of these cases, the climber fell right on the belayer. One case involved distraction. A father was talking at his twelve year old son who was climbing Easy Keyhole (5.2), lost his concentration, and fell. A slightly trickier case, not counted as a climbing statistic, involved a dog lunging at a climber as he was approaching the Trapps. The climber fell, receiving lacerations to the head, arms and face.

Some falls that were reported did not get counted because they are considered "normal"—in that leaders consider falling part of what is to be expected when trying harder routes.

The most interesting accident from this area for this year was one that involved two climbers simul-rappelling. Using the same rope, they had apparently not used a knot, and as he was heavier than she and the rope did not reach the ground, he fell 25 feet to the deck. The other victim fell 40 feet, also off the end of her rope, to the deck. They got away with only a few fractures.

There were no fatalities, and the overall accident rate was down. The number of climbers appears to be constant over the last few years. (Source: From the annual report submitted by the Mohonk Preserve and Jed Williamson)

RAPPELLED OFF END OF ROPE—TECHNIQUE (SPEED AND CONTROL)
North Carolina, Pilot Mountain State Park

On January 1 Nathan Lane (23), with the U.S. Army, was being video taped in the Amphitheater to see how fast he could descend via "Australian Rappel" (face first). Witnesses on the scene described the climber as "out of control" as soon as he began his descent. The climber let go of the rope and fell 30 feet to the base of the route.

He was conscious and alert after the accident. He suffered an open head wound and other facial lacerations. He was evacuated by Pilot Mountain rescue and EMS personnel to NC Baptist Hospital in Winston Salem.

Analysis

The Australian style (also called "butterfly") rappel has no utility in a rock-climbing environment. If is to be undertaken by military personnel or sport rappellers in a climbing setting, it should be done in a slow, controlled descent. A belay would have made the outcome of this incident different. It is not known whether or not the victim was wearing a helmet or gloves. Chances are he was wearing neither. This equipment may have prevented the loss of control and head injury. (Source: Aram Attarian)

RAPPEL ERROR—ANCHOR SLING KNOT CAME UNDONE
North Carolina, Pilot Mountain State Park

On February 1, Joel McSwain (21) fell in the Amphitheater area while attempting to rappel after setting up a top rope anchor. According to his climbing partners, he was beginning his descent when the web sling securing his rappel rope to the anchor "failed." He fell approximately 60 feet to the ground. He sustained extensive trauma, including head injuries, two broken arms, and broken ribs.

Analysis

A self-equalized anchor is only as good as the webbing, cordalette, etc., connecting all points. In this case, the knot (presumably a water knot) securing the webbing came undone. (It was either tied improperly or not tied completely.) Water knots that are used to connect webbing should be checked every time a tied sling is used in an anchor set-up. Water knots have a reputation for loosening themselves. A three-inch tail is considered minimum for this knot.

Consider keeping slings untied when storing them; tie them when needed. Get in the habit of inspecting knots (visual and hands on check). BARK: Before leaving the edge, check your harness: **B**uckle to be sure it is secure and backed through properly; next check your rappel **A**nchor, then your **R**appel/belay device (making sure it's attached correctly and the rope(s) run through it properly; finally, check the **K**nots securing and anchor and belay components.

Anchors can also be tested by stepping into a sling clipped into the masterpoint and bouncing on the anchor. (Make sure you are clipped into a secondary anchor when you do this test!) Also consider using sewn slings for anchor applications or construct a pre-equalized anchor. (Source: Aram Attarian)

FALL ON ROCK—PROTECTION PULLED OUT, LATE START—DARKNESS
North Carolina, Sauartown Mountain

In early May, two male climbers (22 and 21) started a route at Sauartown Mountain late in the day. The leader placed a cam and a stopper prior to clipping the first bolt on route. After clipping the bolt, the pair decided to back off the route because of approaching darkness. The leader decided to down climb the route, removing protection as he did so. The stopper placed earlier was stuck. To remove it the climber placed a cam above the stopper, clipped in and hung on the rope to work on the stopper. "When I yanked the stopper out, the cam popped and I fell, pulling out the cam below me. I landed on my feet and fell sort of in a sitting position on a log at the base of the climb."

The climber sustained a compression fracture of his vertebrae and required an evacuation by Stokes County Mountain Rescue.

Analysis

Starting a route knowing it is going to get dark means you have to understand the route and have the skill to accomplish what needs to be done under these circumstances. A possibility here would have been that instead of down climbing, the climber could have rappelled or lowered off the bolt, removing pro while descending. This practice should only be attempted if the bolt is deemed safe by the climber—as rappelling or lowering off a single bolt is not recommended. (Source: Aram Attarian.)

FALL ON ROCK—HAND-HOLD CAME OFF, INADEQUATE PROTECTION, NO HARD HAT

North Carolina, Crowders Mountain State Park, Gumby Roof

On June 14 at 12:55 p.m. I was informed that Gaston County Sheriffs Department had received a 911 call from a cellular telephone that a climber had fallen in the Gumby Roof area. I proceeded there and met Gaston EMS and Chapel Grove Volunteer Fire department, who had sent in a hasty team to assess victim. I led EMS and extrication team to the site. The victim (30) was placed in a Stokes litter. The terrain is steep and rugged, and required that the litter be belayed and lowered approximate 130 yards down the backside trail to an ambulance.

According to the victim's wife, the rope and carabiner "unclipped" from a fixed bolt as he fell. A nut placed below the bolt also came out, sending D. P. on a 30-foot fall. D. P. landed flat on his back between two boulders. His wife, a nurse, said D. P. had a little difficulty breathing at first, but when she did a head tilt, chin lift, he began breathing normally. He never lost consciousness. D. P. received two stitches to the cut on the back of his head and minor first aid for other cuts and abrasions and was released. (Source: M.P. Edwards, Crowders Mountain State Park)

Analysis

When clipping fixed protection, it is important to consider the orientation of the rope and how it runs through the carabiner. Make sure the rope does not pass over the carabiner gate because it may cause it to unclip accidentally. We can only speculate how the carabiner became detached from the bolt. There is a good chance that if the climber had been wearing a helmet, he may not have needed the stitches. (Source: Aram Attarian)

FALL ON ROCK, EXCEEDING ABILITIES, CLIMBING UNROPED— NO EQUIPMENT

North Carolina, Table Rock Mountain

On July 19 a hiker turned climber fell after scrambling in the vicinity of the Wasp (5.7). He fell approximately 30 to 40 feet, sustaining severe head injury and assorted trauma. After considerable effort he was evacuated by North Carolina Outward Bound School personnel and Burke County EMS. Helicopter evacuation was attempted but aborted due to inadequate LZ.

Analysis
Hikers need to familiarize themselves with the Sierra Club classification system (Class 1-6). Anything beyond the 4th class requires the exclusive use of a rope and specialized equipment, and the knowledge in its use. While not a climbing accident, this is included for the obvious lesson. (Source: Aram Attarian)

FALL ON ROCK, EXCEEDING ABILITIES, NO HARD HAT
North Carolina, Table Rock Mountain, Helmet Buttress

Two climbers a male, B. D. (26) and female, JD (20s) were attempting Helmet Buttress (5.6) on September 2. J. D. was belaying B. D. on the first pitch, which includes a traverse. B. D. fell at the end of the traverse. His feet were level with his last piece of protection (approximately 18 feet out). During the fall the right side of his head struck a tree on the route, resulting in a laceration and a serious skull fracture. B. D. remained conscious as J. D. lowered him to the ground. Two climbers on a nearby route with Wilderness First Responder training arrived almost immediately and begin first aid. J. D. was instructed to maintain a "hands-on stable" position on B. D.'s neck. Once B. D. was stabilized, the other climber ran to the Table Rock Recreation Area parking lot and accessed B. D.'s cell phone, and called 911. The North Carolina Outward Bound School was also notified by a runner (located at the base of the mountain and the local SAR unit), and were first to arrive on the scene. At 12:15 (approximately three hours after the accident) B. D. was evacuated via helicopter to hospital in Asheville, NC. Surgery removed a fist-sized blood clot from B. D.'s skull. He was unconscious and on a respirator for four days. One month later he was approximately 90 percent and recovering.

Analysis
The use of a helmet may have prevented or minimized this injury. B. D. had climbed with a helmet at Table Rock in the past on easier routes. The route was beyond his current level of abilities. (Source: Aram Attarian)

FALL ON ROCK, EXCEEDING ABILITIES, INADEQUATE PROTECTION
North Carolina, Table Rock Mountain, Slipping Into Darkness

On November 1, M. H. (mid 40s) and his two sons (7 and 14) attempted the route Slipping into Darkness (5.9), a variation on Helmet Buttress. M. H. was leading and placed his first piece within the first 50 feet of the climb. He fell well above his last piece of protection prior to the crux and landed on the ground, injuring his back. As a result of the fall M. H., sustained a spinal injury. His seven-year old ran out to the Table Rock Recreation area parking lot where he found a driver to transport him to the North Carolina Outward Bound School Table Rock base camp. NCOBS Mountain Rescue responded, as did Burke County Rescue.

M. H. remained conscious and complained of tingling and numbness in his legs and tenderness in his spine. He was back-boarded and carried out to a waiting helicopter. He was diagnosed as having three cracked vertebrae and small pieces of bone floating around the spinal column. He was operated on in Johnson City, TN, where he himself is an ER physician.

Analysis

Climber should have taken advantage of the numerous opportunities to place gear on this route rather than relying on a single piece. The lead climber should be aware of the belayer's abilities. Belaying the leader requires practice catching and holding a falling leader. Credit is due to the seven-year-old who ran out for help! (Source: Aram Attarian)

FALL ON ROCK, FAILURE TO FOLLOW ROUTE, INADEQUATE BELAY AND PROTECTION, NO HARD HAT, POOR POSITION
Oregon, Smith Rocks

Bill Pesklak (39) and his partner Brian Boshart (25) were working on Titanium Jag, a 5.10b, assigned two stars, an average quality route, by Alan Watts, author of *Climber's Guide to Smith Rock*. Both men had attained a small ledge about 80 feet up the route. With Boshart belaying, Pesklak climbed an estimated 20 feet above the ledge, slipped off, fell on his belayer, tipped off the ledge, fell again striking his head, then slid the remaining 60 feet to rocks below. Pesklak died from massive head injuries. Boshart, with a concussion, back muscle injuries and belay rope burns around his leg, was lowered from the rock six hours after the fall by rescue personnel, hospitalized and released.

Analysis

Titanium Jag has some fixed anchors. Traditional protection gear going up to two inches is suggested. Climbers familiar with the route suggest that Bill Pesklak may have been off line. He had placed one piece about ten feet above his belayer and was working on a second piece when he fell. Brian Boshart was clove hitched with the climbing rope into a two-bolt anchor. He belayed directly to the climber from his harness with an ATC. Both men had discussed his belay position. Boshart stated that he had unclipped his runner from the anchor to move laterally several feet to a position under Bill because of rock fall concern. Brian was able to watch Bill climb. He had locked off the ATC with the rope around his leg as the leader worked on the second piece. Bill fell feet-first onto his belayer, knocking him off the ledge and into a 15-foot pendulum to a point 10 feet below the anchor. Control of the belay was lost; the climber had tipped off the ledge, falling head first then sliding to a stop at the bottom of the climb. Brian remembers the rope playing out through the protection point, which remained on the rock.

Above a belay ledge, experience tells us that the rope should be clipped to a second anchor just above the belayer's head or to the belay anchor, thereby adding friction to the system and pulling the belayer's body weight into the anchor above the ledge while holding a leader fall.

Smith Rock is a highly developed sport climbing area and most routes have been artfully bolted and cleaned of natural debris. Most climbers at Smith Rock do not use helmets on top roped routes. The use of helmets on less developed routes should be a mark of advanced ability and could have saved a life in this instance. The use of a belay device such as the Gri-Gri is a way to stop a fall, uncontrolled by a belayer. Brian believes that use of a Gri-Gri and a helmet might have save Bill's life. (Source: Robert Speik)

AVALANCHE, POOR POSITION
Oregon, Mount Hood, West Crater Rim

The incident took place on Sunday May 31 at 10:05 PDT at the 10,700 foot level on the West Crater Rim route. The occasion was a graduation climb for The Mazamas Basic Climbing Education program.

The party was caught in a large slab avalanche. The fracture occurred about 200 vertical feet below the westernmost summit ridge near the 10,800 foot level. One rope team of three people were caught and swept down a 45–50 degree slope—through the Hot Rocks area and then the gully between Crater Rock and Castle Crags. One person was killed by trauma during the fall, a second person received a fractured pelvis possibly due to the rope breaking between her and the person killed, and a third person on the rope team experienced a fractured ankle. The leader was also briefly caught in the avalanche and experienced an ankle and a shoulder injury.

The avalanche was classified as SS-A0-3 (medium in size relative to its potential path). The crown was 300 feet wide, two feet average depth varying from one to five feet The slope faced southeast and the slide ran from 10,800 feet to the 9,550 foot level, or 1250 vertical feet. The slope angle at the fracture line was 40 degrees. The climbers were engulfed at the 10,700 foot level while traversing a 25–30 degree "ramp."

Stormy, cool weather during much of the preceding week had produced one to two feet of new snow at higher elevations on Mount Hood. Clearing late Saturday allowed sun and rising freezing levels to produce surface snow melt of the upper one to two inches of wind packed snow. Radiation cooling overnight helped briefly stabilize the surface crust. At the time of the accident sun had been warming the slope for about four hours and the air and snow temperatures were rising rapidly. The freezing level was around 10,000 feet. Earlier parties summitted climbing predominantly on the firm crust. However, by mid-morning climbing parties reported knee depth post-holing down to an old crust.

When the group left Timberline Lodge, they observed a hand-written sign, posted in the Forest Service Climbers' Register, stating "HIGH AVALANCHE HAZARD!" The sign had been updated Saturday, May 30 at 8 p.m. by the USFS climbing ranger, only hours before the group set out. It was unusual for such signs to be posted. In fact, this was only the second such sign in seven years.

The leader and other party members observed the sign. The wording of the sign caused questions from and confusion among various party members, some of whom who believed it might have been placed the prior week.

The party left Timberline Lodge at 12:45 a.m. and reached Silcox Hut an hour later, where the assistant leader turned back because of a preexisting injury. One of the basic school students was promoted to be assistant leader. Progress slowed, and it was over three hours later before they left the top of the Palmer ski lift just as the sun was rising. Getting to the base of the steep slope leading to the ridge overlooking Reid Glacier took a further two hours. The ascent of the slope, and a rest to let the Hood River party pass, took about two more hours. Snow conditions deteriorated on the ascent of the steep slope and steps were six to twelve inches deep. The slope that avalanched had been in the sun for about four hours at the time of the release.

On the ascent, the party passed evidence of recent slides on the west side of Crater Rock, a slope similar in aspect to their intended route. The leader probed with his ice ax and was reassured by the firm footing that the snowpack was stable. No hasty snow pits or strength tests were done. The presence of well over 100 climbers on the mountain and another party from Hood River on the West Crater Rim route also mitigated the leaders' concern about avalanche hazard.

After Crater Rock the party traveled in three roped teams. At the time of the avalanche, the leader was traveling unroped just behind the leader of the first rope. A loud crack was heard as the slab released. Within seconds the descending slab disintegrated and overwhelmed the lead rope team and the climb leader. The two trailing rope teams were not involved in the slide. The leader lost his ice ax but was able to stop before being swept down the 45–50 degree slope. The lead rope team was swept through the Hot Rocks area and down to the gully between Crater Rock and Castle Crags.

Two of the rope team were partially buried at the 9,850 foot level, with their rope still attached between them. The third member was completely buried at the 9,650 foot level, the rope having been severed. After dispatching the other rope teams to a safe area, the leader descended the slide path, finding one person buried to his waist and another mostly buried with only her head and arms above the snow. The Hood River party, with two small rope teams and two unroped members were ascending 100–150 feet ahead of the team caught in the slide when the avalanche occurred. This group was on the right (east) flank of the slide. All were just beyond the fracture, except one roped member who was knocked down and carried about 100 feet before his fall was stopped by the self-arrest action of another team member. After this mishap, this party continued to the summit unaware of the nature of the slide they had narrowly escaped.

A USFS climbing ranger, on patrol near the Hogsback, and a member of Portland Mountain Rescue organized a rescue team that descended the debris performing a quick visual and transceiver search. Because the two partly buried climbers reported transceivers were not being used, probe lines were organized. The third climber was uncovered about an hour after burial at a depth of four feet. It was apparent that death resulted from significant injuries suffered in the fall.

Evacuation of the injured victims was accomplished in about three hours by snow cat to Timberline Lodge. Then the most seriously injured person was flown by Life Flight helicopter to Portland. The remainder of the party descended under their own power without any additional leadership.

Analysis

Leadership. The leader was one of the most experienced climb leaders serving as a volunteer for the club. He had climbed several times in Peru and the Himalaya, and had summitted Aconcagua. He had climbed the West Crater Rim route about 15 times and Mount Hood over 50 times. He has been chair of the Climbing Committee. The participants were novice climbers who had completed evening education programs and several weekend outings.

The Route. The West Crater Rim route is frequently ascended. It has longer and steeper sections than the regular Hogsback route. The leader chose the West Crater Rim route about three months previously, intending to avoid the crowds and leave the Hogsback route for another party. The leader preferred this route because it gave "twice the steep climbing and was more enjoyable" than the crowded Hogsback route. Jeff Thomas' *Oregon High Climbing Guide* states: "Be aware that this route is directly in the path of debris falling off Crater Rock, and of any avalanche coming off the slopes above Castle Crags. Huge slides are not uncommon during or right after heavy snowfall, and sometimes in the spring. If conditions are at all shaky, avoid this route."

Transceivers. The climbing ranger commented that most other climbing parties on the mountain that day did not carry avalanche transceivers. Although several people climbing that day owned them, they were left behind. Some of these climbers later remarked that they hadn't considered avalanches to be a problem as it was late in the season and it was such a beautiful day. But in fact, a secondary maximum in monthly Northwest avalanche fatalities occurs in May, similar to the mid-winter Northwest maximums.

Primary causes of the accident:

- The unusually high hazard avalanche conditions resulting from snow loading the previous week during a storm; an old snow crust beneath the new snow; and rapid warming at the time of the release of the avalanche.
- The presence of the party on the West Crater Rim route after the slope had been warmed and destabilized by the sun.

Secondary factors that contributed to the accident:

- The slow pace of the party that resulted in them being on the slope after warming had occurred.
- The leaders' decision to continue on the West Crater Rim route was not questioned because there was no other leader present with sufficient experience.
- The severity of the injuries may have been increased by use of roped team travel. The unroped leader was able to avoid being carried down slope, whereas the rope ensured all three students traveled the avalanche together. The pelvic injuries may have been the result of the rope breaking.
- A confusing warning sign that failed to communicate that the avalanche danger still applied.

- The disturbance of the slope by the Hood River party and the Mazama party may have weakened the slope however the release may have been natural.
- Lack of awareness amongst many climbers on Mount Hood that day about the potential for large slab avalanches "even on nice days."

(Source: From a report by the Incident Response Committee, consisting of John Blanck, Al Cooke, Josh Lockerby, Alan Proffitt, Dave Sauerbrey, Larry Stadler, and Ian Wade)

DISLODGED ROCK—FALL ON ROCK, ROPE SEVERED
Pennsylvania, Delaware Water Gap National Recreation Area, Mount Minsi

On the afternoon of March 26, Daniel O'Malley, Tim Feitzinger, and Jeff Sukenick decided to take advantage of the nice weather to go rock climbing on Mount Minsi. O'Malley and Feitzinger began climbing an established route. Sukenick waited for his companions at the base of the pitch. During the climb, O'Malley evidently dislodged a large rock, which knocked him off the mountain. Feitzinger was in the process of catching him when the climbing rope was severed by the falling boulder. O'Malley fell another 130 to 150 feet to the talus slope below. Sukenick heard the rock hit the ground near him. When he checked it, he came upon O'Malley. Sukenick detected shallow respirations and a soft pulse. He ran down across the talus field to a nearby highway and stood in the road until a vehicle stopped. The driver notified the county dispatch center via her cellular phone. Sukenick then returned to O'Malley and began administering CPR. Rangers and paramedics arrived on scene about 40 minutes after the fall and determined that O'Malley had died. The park's high angle rescue team, comprised of rangers and representatives from the Pennsylvania and New Jersey forestry services and New Jersey state parks, worked themselves into a position above Feitzinger, who was stranded on the cliff, and assisted him in climbing to the top of the rock face. Team members and fire and rescue personnel from several other agencies then removed O'Malley's body via a belayed carry-out down the talus slope in the dark. The response involved about 60 people from seven agencies. (Source: Ed Whitaker, DR, Pennsylvania District)

FALL ON ROCK, EQUIPMENT FAILURE—GRI-GRI
Texas, Barton Creek

The climbing accident concerning the failed Gri-Gri occurred on October 3rd at the cliffs along Barton Creek, near Austin. The climb is called Cyborg, and rated 5.11c; however, I was beyond the crux when I fell. My thigh slammed into a tree 20 feet below the overhang from which my fingers came loose. Blood poured from the numb area as I tried to determine whether my femur was broken or not. I was fortunate that my belayer sacrificed his right palm to slow me down and eventually break my fall. I was also lucky that the cliff overhung beyond the large horizontal ledge, which would have been much more damaging, perhaps even fatal, than the near vertical tree trunk.

Analysis

I am 39 years old and I have been climbing since 1993, with regularity. The one time I spoke with my belayer afterwards, he said later he inspected the Gri-Gri, and he found the rivet to be loose. He suspects this was the cause. I am always very meticulous about double-checking everything, and I remember carefully checking to make sure the Gri-Gri was threaded properly. What went wrong? The Gri-Gri failed. My belayer got a huge rope burn from tightly clenching the rope, and he eventually got the device to lock-up. No bones were broken, and a prescription of Hydrocordon eased the pain, but some lessons were learned.

The more parts there are in a device, the more things that can go wrong. If dirt gets into the Gri-Gri while climbing, it can hinder some of the device's mechanisms. If latch gets snagged in the open position, the rope can slide through. If a part get worn, bent, or cracked, the weakness may not be visible.

No belay device is completely safe. But when I begin climbing again, after I quit limping, I will never again allow anyone to belay me with a Gri-Gri. (Source: Seamus Munroe)

(Editor's Note: This is recorded as Equipment Failure, but it should be noted that I have not received any reports of this device failing until now. There have been reports of individuals using Gri-Gris "upside down," but there is a diagram drawn on the device now.)

RAPPELLED OFF END OF ROPE—NO KNOT AND MISCALCULATION, DARKNESS
Utah, Zion National Park, Moonlight Buttress

On February 18, M. C. and D. G. (ages unknown) began an ascent of Moonlight Buttress (V 5.9 CI). They planned to climb three pitches to the "Rocker Block," fix lines to the ground, then finish the route the following day. As a result of a late start, they didn't get to the anchors until dark. M. C. fixed their first 60 meter rope and rappelled with the second 60 meter rope, stopping at the first set of anchors he came to and well before the end of his line. After fixing the second rope, he began his rappel, expecting to reach the ground. About 50 feet above the ground, he rappelled off the end of his rope. He hit the ground, losing consciousness for three to four minutes. D. G. then rappelled further down the first rope and fixed the second rope to the next set of anchors, continuing to the ground to assist M. C. Amazingly, M. C. suffered only minor bruises and scrapes and was able to walk away from the incident. The team did, however, retrieve their gear the next day and abandon their climb.

Analysis

Darkness was clearly a factor in this incident, since M. C. could not see the next (correct) anchors on his first rappel nor could he see that his rope didn't touch down on his second. However, the accident could have been easily avoided had the topos been consulted, as many of them clearly show three distinct sets of anchors. (It is possible to reach the ground using three 50 meter ropes or two 60 meter ropes.) This combined with the fact that he had too much rope left on his first rappel should have tipped him off to the fact that he was not at the correct anchors. Finally, a simple knot at the end of the rope would have averted the incident entirely. (Source: Tony Thaler, SAR Ranger, Zion National Park)

FALL ON ROCK—CAM HOOK CAME OFF, NO HARD HAT, INADEQUATE PROTECTION
Utah, Zion National Park, Forbidden Wall

On December 27, V. G. (25) and L. E. (20) obtained a backcountry permit to climb Moonlight Buttress. Whether they couldn't find their intended route or changed their minds is unknown, but the two instead began an unnamed/unknown route on Forbidden Wall near the Temple of Sinawava. V. G. began by climbing a 200-foot pitch to a vegetated ledge. The two then hauled their bags and moved across the ledge to the base of their next pitch. V. G., the more experienced climber, began leading out on Leeper cam hooks. About 15 feet on the ledge, V.G. placed a cam, climbed another ten to fifteen feet and placed his second cam. About ten feet above his second cam, and again out on cam hooks, V. G. expressed concern to L. E. about his next hook placement, thinking it suspect. After several minute of tinkering with the placement, V. G. committed his weight to it and the hook blew. He fell more than 20 feet, flipping upside down and striking his head against the wall, losing consciousness. By tugging on the belay line, L. E. was able to reposition V. G. so that he leaned against the wall in a head-up orientation. L. E. then tied him off in place and escaped the belay to get help, using a second lead line tied off to a single cam anchor to rappel from. After scrambling down several hundred feet of scree and then talus, and then crossing the Virgin River, L. E. met another climber, G. A., on the canyon scenic drive. G. A. immediately drove to Zion Lodge and notified park dispatch of the incident while L. E. returned to the scene to assist V. G. Despite a very serious potential hazard, the Zion SAR team safely stabilized V. G., lowered him to the ground, and got him transported to the hospital where he remains in a coma as of this report.

Analysis

Several factors come to light here. First, V. G. decided not to wear a helmet, while insisting the L. E. wear his, since he was the less experienced climber. Second, they were climbing an unknown route of undetermined difficulty. The established routes on Forbidden Wall are some of the hardest and least repeated in the park, some checking in at A4 and A5. The probable lack of sufficient gear likely contribute to the third factor: the question of why V. G. chose not to place reliable protection between the cam-hook he was on and the suspect hook that blew. Finally, L. E.'s failure to construct a safe rappel anchor was almost disastrous. After G. A. summoned help, he returned with L. E. to the belay ledge, ascending the fixed rope. Once Zion SAR team members arrived, G. A. rappelled the line to assist with rescue efforts. SAR team members then ascended the line. So at this point, the single cam anchor had been rappelled on twice and ascended on four times. Upon reaching the ledge, SAR Ranger

K. H. checked the anchor for the other team members and found the nearly expanded single cam behind a fractured block! (Source: From a report by Tony Thaler, SAR Ranger, Zion National Park.)

FALLING ICE, NO HARD HAT, CLIMBING ALONE
Vermont, Smuggler's Notch

On December 30, a man (41) was five or six feet off the ground on a climb when he was struck by a piece of falling ice three feet in diameter. He was knocked off his ice route and fell an additional 30–40 feet down-slope. He suffered lacerations, a concussion and multiple skull fractures.

Fortunately, there were climbers nearby who reported the incident to the Stowe Hazardous Terrain Evacuation team. He was lowered and transported to Burlington. After six weeks in the hospital, he was released, having lost sight in his right eye, but with no other "permanent deficit." The victim called with the rescue team to thank them, and to say that he feels lucky to be alive. (Source: From a report by Neil Van Dyke, Stowe Hazardous Terrain Evacuation Team)

AVALANCHE
Washington, Mount Rainier

This accident occurred as a RMI guided team was descending from the summit. Two rope teams were clipped into the same fixed line when the avalanche occurred. The avalanche caught the first rope team, which pulled two of the anchors on the fixed line. The slide continued unattested also pulling the second rope team down the hill. Finally one anchor (a picket) held at the other end of the fixed line as a few climbers became entangled at the top of the cliffbands. What was left is detailed. One guide and one client were caught on the fixed line above the cliff. Three clients and one guide clung to the top of the cliff, tangled in the rocks and ropes. Three clients dangled below them on a cliff of ice and snow, while the solo client (Nestler) hung below a second cliff band in a waterfall of snowmelt. Nestler died as a result of this exposure.

The Park Service assembled climbing rangers from Camp Schurman and Muir, Mountain Rescue Volunteers, Rainier Mountaineering Guides and helicopters assist with the rescue. On scene, Gauthier along with Rainier Mountaineering Guides Randolf and Eicshner worked to assess the situation. The location was extremely hazardous with 40-degree icy slopes, 20-foot vertical rock bands, exposure to avalanche hang-fire and a 300-foot drop to the glacier below. The danger made it necessary for rescuers to secure the exposed climbers with new ropes and reliable anchors. One of the distressed climbing teams was pendulumed over a refrigerator-sized rotten rock; the other clung to the cliff or dangled on a rope which was frayed to the inner strands and pulled tight over a sharp rock held by one picket! Once new anchors and ropes were established, on scene rescuers negotiated the cliff securing the injured and triaging the patients.

Teams of climbing rangers and guides were inserted with US Army and private helicopters at Ingraham Flats. Some of the rescuers climbed to the accident site to assist with the raising evacuation while another team headed to the base of the cleaver to assist with the lowering of one climber. That climber, Patrick Nestler (29), had fallen substantially farther down the cliff than the others. The fastest evacuation was to lower him off the mountain rather than raise him back to the accident site. New anchors and ropes were set to assist Nestler. However no one had heard from him for over an hour. As the injured were being raised off the cliff above, Nestler was quickly lowered, taken across the bergschrund and evacuated to the helicopter, where he was pronounced dead.

At 1:45 p.m. on June 11th, an independent climber camping at Ingraham Flats overheard screams of distress coming from the Disappointment Cleaver. The climber, using a cell phone, alerted Mount Rainier communications and reported that a snow avalanche had swept two rope teams off "The Nose" of the Cleaver. The initial report indicated that many climbers may be dead and the accident was extremely serious. Off duty climbing ranger Mike Gauthier overheard the emergency announcement on the Park Service radio and responded to the accident from the summit by riding his snowboard down the climbing route. On scene, Gauthier reported that Rainier Mountaineering guided teams had been hit by an avalanche and up to ten climbers (two rope teams) were unsecured on the cliff or unaccounted for.

Climbing rangers remained to clean up and conduct the accident investigation on the following day while additional guides stayed to escort the remaining clients back to Camp Muir.

Efforts to raise the other nine climbers off the cliff and up the slope were hustled as rescuers raced against nightfall. The injuries included: one guide with a severely injured hand, a client with an injured leg and hand, three hypothermic clients, another client with an injured hand, a climber with an injured leg and two shaken but ambulatory climbers. The Chinook helicopter hovered at Ingraham Flats till darkness when the last of the most hypothermic climbers was loaded on board in a liter. All of the injured and a few of the rescuers were flown to Madigan Hospital in Tacoma.

Analysis

This avalanche was described as a "wet, loose snow slide." Released on a 40-degree slope at 11,600 feet, it ran on a layer of isothermal melt-freeze grains when it hit the rope teams at 11,200 feet. The width of the slide when it hit the teams was 38 feet, at a depth of 6–10 inches. Warm temperatures and clear sky (solar radiation) are the most significant weather factors in its cause. At the time of the avalanche the snow pack was in the melt stage of the melt-freeze cycle and the snow grains lacked cohesion. Only a small trigger was needed to start the snow mass moving.

No definite trigger was positively identified at the starting point. However, boot prints and climber activity mark the area on the slope above the traverse. This location is notorious for rock and icefall. Guides fix the traverse because the exposure is great should a climber fall. The guides observed no evidence of any avalanche activity that day. Senior guides commented that the area had no avalanche activity for 20+ years.

Avalanches are not just winter phenomena. Big mountains like Rainier create their own climate and conditions. Different slopes, elevations, angles, and aspects mean new conditions and circumstances. Always consider the possibility of an avalanche, particularly on suspect 25 to 50 degree snow slopes on warm days. Hazards can be assessed by digging a snow pit and checking the slide potential. One can also minimize exposure by moving quickly through hazardous areas. Also consider that humans cause many avalanches. In dangerous areas, make sure your teammates or others are not above—or below! (Source: Mike Gauthier, SAR Ranger, Mount Rainier National Park)

FALL INTO CREVASSE, WEATHER, HYPOTHERMIA
Washington, Mount Rainier

A four-person climbing team had summitted Liberty Ridge on June 14 and became separated (two roped teams of two) during their descent of the Emmons Glacier in severe winds and whiteout conditions. While route finding, the lead climber on the second rope team fell into a crevasse near 13,300 feet. The second climber, Bullard, held the fall in self-arrest for an hour while his partner ascended from the crevasse. Storm conditions intensified and the extended exposure of self-arresting caused Bullard to become wet and hypothermic. The team decided to bivy, but their megamid provided minimal protection from the 60 mph winds and heavy snowfall. They used their cell phone to call the Park and request assistance.

Their partners had safely descended the Emmons and became concerned when their teammates did not arrive at Camp Schurman. They contacted climbing rangers Gottlieb and Kamencik about the same time the White River Ranger Station received the telephone call. Inclement weather prevented assistance that evening and a rescue was organized for the following morning based on reports of improving weather. A three-person team (the two climbing rangers and one of the party's team members) would climb from Camp Schurman while an Army Chinook helicopter would attempt to fly another team of rangers to the reported location. Cloud conditions improved, but extremely high winds prevented a helicopter insertion. Aerial reconnaissance helped to guide the ground team, which climbed through deep snow and fierce winds, sometimes on their hands and knees, to the climber's bivy.

The rescue team found both climbers hypothermic, suffering from exposure and dehydration. Efforts to evade the wind and light the stove proved futile and the aggressive rewarming was needed for one member. The weather continued to improve and after a few hours the climbers and rescuers were able to descend under their own power back to Camp Schurman.

Analysis

Extremely fierce weather including whiteouts, high winds and substantial snowfall are not uncommon on Mount Rainier during the summer months. Weather may be the largest contributing factor to accidents, rescues, and searches. Inclement weather contributed to this team becoming split, but stronger efforts should always be made to stay together during such conditions. The immediate assistance of their teammates may have significantly changed the outcome of the initial crevasse fall. It is also important to note that three other climbing teams reported passing the stranded climbers while descending Liberty Cap. They offered assistance however the two-person Bullard party declined, perhaps feeling their situation was not urgent at the time. (Source: Mike Gauthier, SAR Ranger, Mount Rainier National Park)

FALL ON SNOW/ICE
Washington

Two climbers requesting a rescue for a third team member on Liberty Ridge contacted Mount Rainier National Park early on June 16th. The injured climber, Talbot (60), had severely broken his lower leg during a 200-foot fall while descending the route. Unable to down-climb, his partners stabilized him at 10,000 feet on the ridge before going for help.

NPS climbing rangers assembled a rescue team and flew to the Carbon Glacier. The rescue team ascended 1,000 feet of technical mountaineering terrain to provide emergency care. Talbot was lowered 900 feet on 40 to 60 degree snow and ice slopes to the glacier at the base of Liberty Wall. There, a helicopter could land and Talbot was transported to the Park Service heli-base where an ambulance awaited. The rescue took four hours round trip.

Analysis

There have been a number of injuries like this on Liberty Ridge and similar mountaineering routes, which are notorious for loose and dangerous snow, rock and ice conditions that change rapidly depending on the weather, and altitude. One day the snow may be hard, the next it may be sugar. Climbers should also be prepared for strenuous physical exercise with heavy packs and technical terrain. These difficulties, coupled with altitude and the severe weather, make Rainier a place where simple accidents often turn into large emergencies. (Source: Mike Gauthier, SAR Ranger, Mount Rainier National Park)

HAPE AND HACE
Washington, Mount Rainier

While spending the night on the summit of Mount Rainier, off duty climbing rangers Gauthier and Patterson were contacted by the leader of a scientific research team, who informed them that one of his team members was suffering from mountain sickness. The rangers found Haley in his tent, disoriented, suffering from slurred speech, and unable to support himself. Team members indicated that his condition had deteriorated significantly in the previous 15 minutes and that his behavior was abnormal. A helicopter was requested, but nightfall and altitude prevented a safe response. Within 15 minutes of the initial assessment, Haley became unconscious and unresponsive. Assisted rescue breathing was provided throughout the night while a climbing team from Camp Muir attempted to reach the summit with oxygen, but newly formed crevasses and whiteout conditions prevented their efforts and Haley was evacuated shortly after sunrise by an Army Chinook helicopter and flown to Madigan Hospital. He was unconscious and in critical condition.

Analysis

Haley suffered from High Altitude Cerebral and Pulmonary Edema (HACE and HAPE.) Although Haley was part of a team that had spent four days and three nights transporting gear to the summit, he still reported headaches and a feeling of nausea. Haley also commented that he did not drink much water on his summit day. By the time his condition had deteriorated seriously enough to alert his team members, Haley was immobile, so a safe, rapid descent was out of the question.

Climbers on Mount Rainier frequently feel the effects of altitude sickness, but most do not get seriously sick because they descend to sea level before many of the medical complications arise. Acclimatization on Rainier is difficult because most climbers go from sea level to 14,411 feet in less than 24 hours. Parties that expect to stay at altitude should have a systematic plan of acclimatization. Anyone exhibiting or complaining of the signs and symptoms of acute mountain sickness should be taken seriously. A rapid descent is the best treatment. It is imperative that team members watch each other. It is not uncommon for climbers to dismiss their symptoms as other maladies and push on. (Source: Mike Gauthier, SAR Ranger, Mount Rainier National Park)

SLIP ON SNOW—UNABLE TO SELF-ARREST, UNROPED, POOR POSITION, INSTRUCTOR NOT FAMILIAR WITH ROUTE
Washington, North Cascades, Saska Peak

While participating in a climb of Saska Peak on Day 17 of a Pacific Crest Outward Bound sea/mountain course, a female student (c. 20) slipped and fell on a small snow slope and was unable to self-arrest. She fell 450 feet and came to rest on a rock. The instructors quickly moved down to the site after stabilizing the rest of the group. The instructors from another group were summoned when they passed by the scene with their patrol and radio contact and a request for helicopter assistance was made with the U.S. Forest Service. Primary and secondary surveys were completed and a litter was constructed for evacuation.

While the instructors were waiting for a helicopter with winching capabilities, the student went into cardiac and respiratory arrest. CPR was performed, but was to no avail. The helicopter was able to carry out the evacuation, but the student did not survive.

Analysis

An internal and external review were conducted, and the conclusions were the same. The combination of reliance on self-arrest, no experience in self-arrest with a heavy pack, an inadequate runout, and no fixed line or belay were the key factors in this accident.

It was also noted that the instructors were not familiar with the route, as no reconnaissance had been conducted. Considering the injuries to the student, the geographic location, and resources, nothing more could have been done to change the outcome of the accident once the fall began. The instructors' response to the emergency was deemed to be thorough and professional. (Source: From reports prepared by Outward Bound and the External Review Team.)

FALLING ROCKS—DISLODGED BY CLIMBER
Washington, North Cascades, Mount Logan

On Labor Day weekend, Silas Wild and I climbed the east ridge of Thunder Peak, a satellite of Mount Logan in the North Cascades. On Saturday, we hiked over Easy Pass, down Fisher Creek and up a steep forested slope to a 5200 foot lake northeast of Logan. Beckey's guide recommends this route to approach Logan's Banded Glacier. From a camp above the lake, on Sunday morning we crossed a 7040 foot col to reach the base of our route.

The 2000 foot ridge has two notches, at 7500 and 8000 feet. We rappelled eighty feet into the first notch. We found some nylon fibers at the rappel horn, indicating that someone had been there before. The route had no previous reported ascent, so we don't know whether the earlier party was successful or whether they retreated from this point.

The crux of the climb was a 5.7 pitch out of the first notch. From there to the second notch, the ridge was mostly low class 5 on solid rock. The route has great views of Ragged Ridge, the Arriva-Black group, the Douglas Glacier and the north face of Mount Goode. The second notch had a short rappel and a rotten gully, but the rock improved above it. We reached the 8800 foot summit at 4 p.m., about ten hours from camp. Mount Logan and the Banded Glacier dominated the view. We noted icebergs floating in the lake at the foot of the glacier.

The descent was class 3 down-climbing, then a gentle talus descent along the north ridge of the peak. We rappelled 150 feet from the low point of the ridge, then descended snow, slabs and steep moraine back to the basin where we had camped. Near the base of the moraine, not more than twenty feet from flat ground, Silas dislodged a loose boulder. This started a chain reaction of boulders tumbling underfoot and above him. I watched horrified as he fell and was overwhelmed by crashing rocks. When the avalanche stopped, I scrambled down and found him lying on his back, his legs and right arm buried, and a suitcase-sized rock on his torso. Silas wailed to get it off, saying that he couldn't breathe. I strained to lift it for a few seconds, then with Silas pushing with his good left arm, we shifted it clear.

Next I removed the rocks burying his right arm. After loosening his pack straps, he miraculously wriggled free. His legs had been caught and spared by a pocket between the boulders. Even more amazing, after his pain subsided some and we assessed his condition, was that he could walk. His right shin had a one inch gash, both legs were bruised and sore, and his right arm was swollen, but that was about it.

He hobbled a hundred yards to good camping site and I fetched our overnight gear from our previous camp in the twilight. We got him into his sleeping bag and discussed having me hike out for a helicopter the next day.

On Monday morning, Silas was feeling better and thought he could hike out. We loaded the heavy gear into one pack, which I carried, and put sleeping bags, bivi sack, food and a head lamp in the other pack for him to carry. Since his right arm was not usable, I lowered him with a rope a few times down the steep forest. After we reached the Fisher Creek trail, I hiked ahead to Colonial Campground, 13 miles away. Tired, hurting, and walking slowly, Silas spent that night on the trail. But he was moving steadily under his own power when two rangers and I found him early the next morning.

Back in Seattle the doctors reported a broken wrist, bruises, and a cut on his shin that should heal without stitches. Silas and I both gained more respect for the dangers of moraines. I've had a chance to ponder the problems of self sufficiency and accident response in remote wilderness areas. (Source: Lowell Skoog)

AVALANCHE, POOR POSITION
Wyoming, Grand Teton National Park, Mount Owen

On the evening of April 22, Ranger Renny Jackson received a phone call from Jackson resident Christian Beckwith. According to Beckwith, his friend Stephen Koch (29) had not returned from a solo snowboard descent on Mount Owen. Koch had planned to depart the Taggart Trailhead early on April 22, bicycle to south Jenny Lake, ski up Cascade Canyon, then climb Mount Owen via the north face. He would then attempt the first snowboard descent via the Northeast Snowfields and return that same day. As Koch is a very experienced mountaineer and snowboarder, Beckwith's level of concern was significant.

On the morning of April 23, rangers confirmed that Koch's vehicle was still parked in the Taggart parking lot. At 0915, a helicopter search was initiated for Koch with myself (Mark Magnuson) and Renny Jackson on board. Tracks were followed up Cascade Canyon and into the Owen Cirque below the north face. A pair of cached skis were seen midway up the lower snowfield, with a boot track traversing back and forth across the slope above, leading up to the face. At 0950, pilot Ken Johnson spotted Koch in the main snowfield below the north face, sitting at the base of a large boulder. Koch was waving. Johnson performed a toe-in landing/hover several hundred feet above Koch, and Jackson exited the aircraft. He went directly to Koch to assess injuries. Johnson and I then flew back over Cascade Canyon to make radio contact with ranger Rick Perch, the Incident Commander. After updating Perch on the status of Koch and resource needs, Johnson returned to the scene, and I departed the aircraft with our gear.

Koch was found in a sitting position, with his climbing harness beneath his buttocks. He was wearing light gear (neck gaiter around the head, goggles, medium-weight long-sleeve North Face capilene shirt, medium-weight long underwear, guide pants, gloves, and double plastic boots). He had no additional equipment with him as his pack had been lost in the slide. Koch was dehydrated and hypothermic, but conscious, alert, and conversant. He had extensive wounds visible to his face and head, was spitting up small amounts of blood, and was complaining primarily of pain in both knees, neck, and back. He stated that both knees were "blown."

We began efforts to warm Koch by providing additional clothing, then continued to further assess his injuries. Additional equipment was delivered to the scene via long line/sling load. A cervical collar was placed on his neck, and high flow oxygen was administered.

Rangers Andy Byerly, Scott Guenther, Dan Burgette, and Chris Harder were flown into the scene, along with additional equipment. Rewarming of Koch continued with heat bags placed under the arms, in the groin, and on the abdomen. With concurrence from medical control (Dr. Rick McKay), Koch was secured on a scoop stretcher in full cervical-spinal immobilization. A splint was placed on his right leg and he was moved into an evac-bag inside the litter. With orders from Dr. McKay, I started an IV of warmed Normal Saline at 1000 cc/hour and administered 25 grams of D-50 (dextrose).

A landing platform was shoveled into the snow approximately 200 feet above and Koch was raised via z-rig to that location. Johnson returned with the helicopter, landed, and Koch was placed inside the aircraft. I flew with Koch to St. John's Hospital, arriving at 1237. Johnson returned to the scene, and by 1530 all personnel and equipment had been flown from the mountain.

Koch's injuries included a fracture-dislocation of the right knee with associated tears of all supporting ligaments, ACL and MCL tears in the left knee, fractures of two lower thoracic vertebrae, pulmonary contusions, chipped tooth with possible misalignment of the mandible, and multiple abrasions, contusions, and lacerations over the body.

Analysis

The following interview with Stephen Koch took place in the St. John's Hospital emergency room on April 23, with additional follow-up questions the next day after he had been admitted.

According to Koch, he departed the Taggart Trailhead area at 0250 on April 22, then bicycled to south Jenny Lake. He stashed his bike at the Teton Boating cabins then skied around the edge of Jenny Lake and up lower Cascade Canyon. He crossed Cascade Creek below the Owen Cirque and began the steep ascent toward the base of the north face. Along the way he cached his skis and began kicking steps up the snow. About the 9,000 foot level, he stopped and left a stuff sack containing a headband, goggles, two high energy food bars, and camera on the downhill side of a large boulder. Koch continued kicking steps up the slope and, due to the late morning hour and avalanche activity that was starting, changed his line of ascent by moving left on the face. He was now using two ice tools and, having aborted use of crampons due to snow balling up on the bottoms, continued kicking steps. He said as the slopes above continued to warm, debris began coming down from the Northeast Snowfields. He again adjusted his plan, with thoughts of waiting at the Koven Col to reassess conditions.

About 1050, an avalanche passed by to his right, followed by a second, larger slide. Koch thought this would miss him as well. However, after taking two steps to his left, he was swept off his feet. Koch said he was thrown down the face in a very violent fall, tumbling over at least two rock cliffbands of about 15 feet in height. After sustaining significant multiple injuries in a 2,000 foot fall, he came to rest at the bottom of the face. Snow had packed his mouth and throat, requiring a struggle to clear his airway and breathe. One ice tool in his pack and attached snowboard were lost in the fall.

Realizing that he now lay in the middle of the primary avalanche track below the north face, Koch hobbled several hundred feet down and across the slope to a safer location, then collapsed. Unable to continue, he drifted in and out of consciousness for the next three to four hours, until the sun moved behind the peak. With temperatures dropping, he began glissading down the slope on his left hip and then his back. He continued a very slow descent until he reached his gear cache at the boulder. It was here that he spent the night, sitting on his climbing harness.

Koch planned to sit out the night, feeling relatively confident that he would be reported overdue and that the Jenny Lake Rangers would be responding the following day. He said he had planned to wait until about 1130 for rescue, at which time he would continue his attempt to descend. In hindsight, Koch said he would have benefited from wearing a helmet and, while he thought he had picked a safe line up the face, realized that he was behind schedule and subject to the hazards of changing conditions. He did not anticipate that debris from above would affect him on his adjusted line of ascent. He noted that he was still climbing in the shade, but sun had already been warming the upper slopes. Koch expressed extreme gratitude for having survived the accident and for the rescue effort that ensued. (Source: Mark Magnuson, SAR Coordinator)

(Editor's Note: In the "Jackson Hole News," April 29, 1998, Koch is quoted as saying that he survived, he believes, because of his will to live. Also, he said, "Too much to do. Babies to have. It's a sign. I've got more work to do on this earth—helping others, especially since I've been helped so much." His recovery has gone well.)

FALL ON ICY ROCK—BLOWN OVER BY WIND
Wyoming, Grand Teton National Park, Grand Teton

On June 25, James McDonald, Larry Susanka and Dan Sola (38) were attempting to climb the Exum Ridge of the Grand Teton in icy conditions with a storm in progress. Around 1430 Sola fell about ten feet while leading the Friction Pitch. Sola was wearing crampons on the iced rock, but was caught by a strong gust of wind and blown over backwards. He had protection below him, but still hit the belay ledge, dislocating his right shoulder and injuring his ankle. Susanka used a cell phone to call 911 and was connected to Ranger Tom Kimbrough at the Jenny Lake Ranger Station. Susanka asked for route information, but stated that the party would try to descend without help. Park Medical Control, Lanny Johnson, PA, was contacted and called Susanka to talk them through the reduction of the dislocated shoulder. When Johnson reached them by cell phone, the reduction had already been accomplished. The group rappelled and down-climbed the Exum Ridge, occasionally calling for route information. They reached Wall Street, the end of the most technical part of the descent, at 1840. Continuing down, they arrived at the Lower Saddle at 2130.

When this group left the Lower Saddle to climb the Grand Teton at 0445, a fourth member of the party, Jack Hicks, elected not to climb. He remained at the Saddle, and when tents began to be blown down by strong winds, he broke the window of the Ranger Hut to gain access to better shelter. He also contacted Mike Detmer, a ham radio operator in Jackson, to let the Park know that weather conditions were severe and that he was worried about the other members of his group. Detmer continued to assist with communications until the climbers were safe at the Lower Saddle.

Susanka and Sola continued their descent to the Lupine Meadows Trailhead during the night of June 25. They arrived at the trailhead at 0230 on June 26. Hicks and McDonald spent the night at the Saddle, returning to the trailhead by 1400. (Source: Tom Kimbrough, SAR Ranger)

FALL ON SNOW, INADEQUATE EQUIPMENT, CLIMBING ALONE
Wyoming, Grand Teton National Park, Disappointment Peak

On July 11, Joe Zitomer and Melynda Cable stopped at the Jenny Lake Rescue Cache to report possible cries for help coming from Disappointment Peak. Zitomer and Cable had hiked to Amphitheatre Lake, arriving between 1500 and 1530, when they heard the cries. They described them as male and coming from the cliffs above the lake to the south. They heard the cries for a period of about 30 minutes and confirmed in their own minds that they were indeed calls for help. While at the lake, they ran into a party of two males who also heard the cries. Zitomer and Cable then hiked back down the trail to make the report.

At 1655 park dispatch received a cellular phone call from off-duty naturalist Jeff Hancock. Hancock reported an injured climber who had fallen 120 feet in the ice couloir above Amphitheatre Lake and sustained serious injuries (bilateral ankle fractures and head and chest trauma).

The NPS/USFS contract helicopter piloted by Ken Johnson departed Lupine Meadows at 1715 with rangers Ron Johnson and Bill Culbreath on board. A recon flight of Disappointment Peak located the injured climber in the snow couloir along the east side of the Lake Ledges Route. Johnson was able to land the helicopter several hundred feet above the accident site and Culbreath and Johnson descended to the scene, arriving at 1738. Rangers Bill Alexander and Jim Springer were flown to the same landing zone with additional medical and rescue gear and also descended to the scene.

Following a patient assessment and consultation with medical control Lanny Johnson, Gale Long's suspected injuries (wrist fractures, femur fracture, cervical-spinal, and head and chest trauma) were stabilized. Given the mechanism of fall and the nature of Long's injuries, along with other evacuation alternatives, a decision was made to shorthaul Long from the accident scene to Lupine Meadows.

At 1904, the patient was transferred to NPS Ambulance Medic 1 and was en route to St. John's Hospital, arriving there at 1933. Long was admitted with extremity fractures, torn tendons in his thumb (requiring surgery), rib fractures, multiple facial lacerations requiring sutures, and abrasions and contusions over the entire body.

Analysis

On July 12, I interviewed Gale Long (56) in his room at St. John's Hospital. According to Long, he arrived in Grand Teton National Park on July 10 and left the Lupine Meadows Trailhead at 1300. He spent Friday night bivouacked on the hill above Amphitheatre Lake intending to climb Disappointment Peak the following day via the Lake Ledges route. Long said he scoped the route from the valley prior to his departure and, given the amount of snow observed on the peak, elected not to take an ice ax.

He left his camp at 0900 on July 10 and ascended the Lake Ledges route, arriving on the summit about 1300. Long said the snow on the way up was soft, providing good step kicking. He carried two ski poles with him. He started back down from the summit by 1315, retracing his route of ascent. Upon arriving at the top of the Lake Ledges route (1400 to 1430), the snow was still soft. He planned to traverse the top of the snow couloir from south to north and, as he did, he slipped, the snow being significantly harder as he traversed to the north, into the shade. Long described his subsequent fall as happening extremely fast, taking him (airborne at times) over snow and bands of rock. He finally shot off the snow and landed on the top edge of a large chockstone, preventing what may have been a fatal fall over a steeper cliff.

Long said he was wet (lying in running water), bleeding, and disoriented and unable to use his right leg. He moved up to the south side of the gully, seeking a drier location. He attempted to make voice contact with persons below who, having heard his cries for help, climbed to his location, arriving about one hour later. This group included a first-year physician and an EMT.

Having climbed for 25 years with numerous routes in the Teton Range (the complete Exum, East Ridge of the Grand Teton, and the East Ridge and Northeast Snow Fields of Owen), Long described himself as an experienced mountaineer. He said his principal mistake was not taking his ice ax, thinking that he could bypass the snow. He said he also failed to account for the snow being harder on the descent, the route being in early afternoon shadows with the setting sun. Long said he had not climbed the route before but had studied it in a guide book.

Long, an employee of the Bureau of Land Management, was warned regarding his failure to obtain the required overnight backcountry permit. (Source: Mark Magnuson, SAR Coordinator)

FALL ON ROCK—PROBABLY LOOSE ROCKS
Wyoming, Grand Teton National Park, Baxter's Pinnacle

On August 14 around 1745, Jason Coles reported an injured climber near the base of the rappel at Baxter's Pinnacle. He stated the victim fell 120 feet and sustained a head injury and numerous other injuries. Rangers conducted a 2,000 foot technical lowering to the Cascade Canyon horse trail. He was placed on the wheel litter and taken to the Jenny Lake west shore boat dock, placed on the concessions boat and taken across to the east shore boat dock. Medic I picked him up and took him to Lupine Meadows where he was airlifted by helicopter to the Eastern Idaho Regional Medical Center.

The victim, Larry Kruse (40), sustained numerous fractures and abrasions.

He sustained a concussion, but no serious head injury. He is unable to recall any of the events before or after the accident.

Analysis

Jeff Steinmetz, Kruse's partner, stated the following. We reached the top of Baxter's Pinnacle, and Larry rappelled off first. Kruse called up that he was off rappel and as I started clipping in, I heard him yell, "Rock." About four seconds later I heard what sounded like rockfall. I called to Larry but he didn't answer. I rappelled down to the notch and didn't see Larry. I called but received no reply. I pulled the rappel rope and started to down climb the descent gully. After climbing down about 80 feet I heard him moaning. I climbed to a tree about 30 feet above him and set up an anchor. I rappelled down to him and clipped him into the rope due to his precarious position. I started yelling for help, and two climbers rappelled down from Baxter's to help. I didn't see Larry fall and think he may have rappelled into the gully to the west of the notch instead of stopping at the notch.

Steinmetz stated that Larry had been climbing for 12–15 years. He is a solid 5.10 leader. He has climbed in Yosemite, Red Rocks, and many other places but never in Grand Teton National Park. (Source: Mark Magnuson, SAR Coordinator)

(Editor's Note: Though we don't know the exact cause of Kruse's fall, this accident is worth noting to provide a warning for even the most experienced who climb and descend Baxter's Pinnacle. Loose rock, especially on the descent, is a known hazard here, and has caused many injuries or near misses.)

FALLING/DISLODGED ROCK
Wyoming, Wind River Range, Easy Day Peak

On August , 9 at 1100, while following the first Pitch of the North Face route on Easy Day Peak (11,660 feet), Mark Gallagher pulled a large block off onto himself, and sustained injuries to both of his lower legs. His climbing partner, David Oka, lowered Gallagher to a ledge, fixed him to an anchor, and then rappelled to provide assistance. Two of Gallagher's companions, who were at the group's campsite at Shadow Lake, came up with first aid and other equipment to help with the rescue effort. Together they managed to splint one of Gallagher's legs and lower him off the technical portion of the climb. At this point Oka ran out to Big Sandy trailhead and then drove to Big Sandy Lodge and reported the accident via cellular telephone to Sublette County Sheriff Hank Ruland. Sheriff Ruland, IC for the incident, then requested the assistance of Grand Teton National Park SAR personnel from the Jenny Lake subdistrict about 1800. The initial report of the accident indicated that the injured party was 500–1,000 vertical feet above Shadow Lake and at least one technical climbing pitch up on the route. Three Jenny Lake rangers (Larson, Byerly, and Guenther) along with the Bridger/Teton helitack foreman (Stailey) were flown to Shadow Lake, where the injured climber and his party were spotted during an aerial reconnaissance. All of the equipment required to accomplish both technical and non-technical lowerings as well as the emergency medical and helicopter shorthaul gear to stabilize and evacuate the patient were on board the aircraft. Due to weight restrictions and the high altitude, the helitack crew member was flown to the 8,000 foot level and dropped off. Rangers Larson, Byerly, and Guenther were then flown to a meadow below Easy Day Peak, setting down at 2030.

Once on the ground, the rangers were met by a member of the party and apprised of Gallagher's injuries and overall condition. The rangers then climbed up to Gallagher's location, arriving at 2100, and met the rescue party at the start of the non-technical terrain. After assessing the patient's condition the group began a series of non-technical lowerings down the slope. Gallagher was placed on a backboard and belayed down five rope lengths as the rangers and other climbers carried the litter. At 2215 the patient and rescuers arrived at the meadow below the peak, and a decision was made to set up camp.

As camp was being set up, a more thorough assessment revealed a possible fracture of the right tibia, a laceration on the right foot, and a laceration/avulsion of the medial left ankle. The injuries were cleaned and rebandaged and the right leg resplinted. A request was made to Medical Advisor Lanny Johnson for the antibiotic Ancef, due to the nature of his wounds. Permission was granted, an IV was inserted, and 1.5 grams of Ancef were given with no complications.

At 0855 the following morning Helicopter 6AH picked up the patient and ranger Byerly and they were flown to Pinedale Airport, where they were met by the Pinedale ambulance. Helicopter 6AH then returned for rangers Larson and Guenther. The patient was taken to the clinic in Pinedale, then transported to St. John's Hospital in Jackson. X-rays found a comminuted fracture of the right tibia, a hairline fracture just distal to the right knee, and no fractures to the left leg. All SAR personnel were back in Grand Teton National Park by 1500 on August 10. (Source: Renny Jackson, SAR Ranger)

(Editor's Note: It wasn't too many years ago that a rescue like this in the Wind River Range would have been more difficult and complicated. It probably would have taken several days, and would have been without the benefit of antibiotics.)

FALL ON ROCK, CLIMBING ALONE
Wyoming, Grand Teton National Park, Symmetry Spire

On October 12 at 1600, I received a call from Barbara Lachmar of Logan, UT, who stated that her husband Tom Lachmar (45) had not returned from a climbing trip to the Tetons. She was only able to give me information on the vehicle he was driving, and that he had left on the night of the 10th with a plan to climb the next day and drive back that evening.

I called Teton dispatch and requested that a road patrol ranger begin looking for Lachmar's vehicle at the numerous trailheads in the South District of the park. Additionally, I requested that the Permits Office search the computer database for any record of a backcountry overnight permit or a Voluntary Mountaineering Registration. The vehicle was located at the String Lake trailhead at 1650.

At 1737, I requested that the Bridger-Teton contract helicopter report to the Lupine Meadows heli-base. During the final hour of remaining daylight, I at least wanted to conduct an aerial reconnaissance of the primary hiking routes available from this trailhead.

In the rapidly diminishing daylight, about 1815, the subject was found in the upper reaches of the couloir immediately west of the Southwest Ridge of Symmetry Spire. We were able to confirm that he was injured, and made the decision to attempt to insert one rescuer and then short-haul the climber out via "screamer" suit. The operation was completed by 1855, and Lachmar was transferred to a ground ambulance for evaluation of his injuries. Lachmar was given strong recommendation to seek initial treatment at St. John's Hospital, but he declined, and was taken to his car. He drove home and was admitted to Logan Regional Hospital, where he received treatment for a fractured left clavicle and three separate fractures to his pelvis.

Analysis

Lachmar's intention was to do a day climb of the East Ridge of Symmetry Spire, and then descend via the rappels from the notch on the upper portion of the Southwest Ridge. He had successfully completed the first long rappel and was in the process of down climbing to the second rappel when he fell about "five to seven feet." The accident occurred about 1545. He spent the night there, and then started making his way down the next day.

Climbers will continue to be encouraged to let someone responsible know exactly where they intend to go and when they are expected to return. Lachmar was well equipped for a day climb. He is fortunate that the injuries he sustained were not life threatening. (Source: From a report by SAR Ranger Renny Jackson)

TABLE I
REPORTED MOUNTAINEERING ACCIDENTS

	Number of Accidents Reported		Total Persons Involved		Injured		Fatalities	
	USA	CAN	USA	CAN	USA	CAN	USA	CAN
1951	15		22		11		3	
1952	31		35		17		13	
1953	24		27		12		12	
1954	31		41		31		8	
1955	34		39		28		6	
1956	46		72		54		13	
1957	45		53		28		18	
1958	32		39		23		11	
1959	42	2	56	2	31	0	19	2
1960	47	4	64	12	37	8	19	4
1961	49	9	61	14	45	10	14	4
1962	71	1	90	1	64	0	19	1
1963	68	11	79	12	47	10	19	2
1964	53	11	65	16	44	10	14	3
1965	72	0	90	0	59	0	21	0
1966	67	7	80	9	52	6	16	3
1967	74	10	110	14	63	7	33	5
1968	70	13	87	19	43	12	27	5
1969	94	11	125	17	66	9	29	2
1970	129	11	174	11	88	5	15	5
1971	110	17	138	29	76	11	31	7
1972	141	29	184	42	98	17	49	13
1973	108	6	131	6	85	4	36	2
1974	96	7	177	50	75	1	26	5
1975	78	7	158	22	66	8	19	2
1976	137	16	303	31	210	9	53	6
1977	121	30	277	49	106	21	32	11
1978	118	17	221	19	85	6	42	10
1979	100	36	137	54	83	17	40	19
1980	191	29	295	85	124	26	33	8
1981	97	43	223	119	80	39	39	6
1982	140	48	305	126	120	43	24	14
1983	187	29	442	76	169	26	37	7
1984	182	26	459	63	174	15	26	6
1985	195	27	403	62	190	22	17	3
1986	203	31	406	80	182	25	37	14
1987	192	25	377	79	140	23	32	9
1988	156	18	288	44	155	18	24	4
1989	141	18	272	36	124	11	17	9
1990	136	25	245	50	125	24	24	4
1991	169	20	302	66	147	11	18	6
1992	175	17	351	45	144	11	43	6
1993	132	27	274	50	121	17	21	14

	Number of Accidents Reported		Total Persons Involved		Injured		Fatalities	
	USA	CAN	USA	CAN	USA	CAN	USA	CAN
1994	158	25	335	58	131	25	27	5
1995	168	24	353	50	134	18	37	7
1996	139	28	261	59	100	16	31	6
1997	158	35	323	87	148	24	31	13
1998	138	24	281	55	281	18	20	1
Totals	4952	726	8982	1534	4383	577	1178	249

TABLE II

	1951–1997			1998		
Geographical Districts	Number of Accidents	Deaths	Total Persons Involved	Number of Accidents	Deaths	Total Persons Involved
Canada						
Alberta	383	112	842	13	1	28
British Columbia	260	103	579	4	0	9
Yukon Territory	33	26	73	0	0	0
Ontario	33	8	61	0	0	0
Quebec	29	8	62	0	0	0
East Arctic	8	2	21	0	0	0
West Arctic	1	1	2	0	0	0
Practice Cliffs[1]	13	2	18	7	0	18
United States						
Alaska	385	154	596	12	3	26
Arizona, Nevada Texas	64	11	121	9	2	17
Atlantic–North	710	100	1203	27	0	45
Atlantic–South	67	20	105	13	1	28
California	971	236	2025	24	0	45
Central	120	13	193	1	0	1
Colorado/Oklahoma	613	181	1053	28	7	53
Montana, Idaho South Dakota	63	25	97	1	0	1
Oregon	140	68	333	4	3	10
Utah, New Mexico	113	39	202	4	1	9
Washington	926	271	1657	8	3	32
Wyoming	476	106	875	7	0	12

[1]This category includes bouldering, as well as artificial climbing walls, buildings, and so forth. These are also added to the count of each state and province, but not to the total count, though that error has been made in previous years.

(Editor's Notes: 1) The Practice Cliffs category has been removed from the U.S. data. 2) Last year, nine significant reports (eight in Colorado and one in California) came in after publication. They included three fatalities. Cumulative data reflect these incidents in Tables II and III.)

TABLE III

	1951–97 USA	1959–97 CAN.	1998 USA	1998 CAN.
Terrain				
Rock	3572	427	102	18
Snow	2081	312	28	1
Ice	190	100	8	4
River	13	3	0	0
Unknown	22	7	0	1
Ascent or Descent				
Ascent	3169	458	89	11
Descent	1938	310	49	13
Unknown[3]	247	4	0	0
Immediate Cause				
Fall or slip on rock	2471	231	77	8
Slip on snow or ice	808	165	20	1
Falling rock, ice or object	496	110	10	4
Exceeding abilities	418	27	22	0
Avalanche	256	107	4	2
Exposure	237	13	4	0
Illness[1]	280	21	7	0
Stranded	267	8	8	3
Rappel Failure/Error[2]	208	38	13	2
Loss of control/glissade	168	16	1	0
Fall into crevasse/moat	132	41	4	0
Failure to follow route	126	27	5	0
Nut/chock pulled out	101	3	9	0
Piton pulled out	84	12	2	0
Faulty use of crampons	69	5	1	0
Lightning	39	7	0	0
Skiing	48	9	0	0
Ascending too fast	43	0	2	0
Equipment failure	7	2	4	0
Other[3]	203	24	86	4
Unknown	59	8	1	0
Contributory Causes				
Climbing unroped	902	150	10	1
Exceeding abilities	834	175	4	9
Inadequate equipment/clothing	552	71	7	1
Placed no/inadequate protection	492	75	38	4
Weather	378	57	10	0
Climbing alone	325	57	4	0
No hard hat	247	24	13	1
Nut/chock pulled out	181	16	4	0
Darkness	118	19	4	0
Party separated	100	17	3	0
Piton pulled out	84	10	0	0

	1951–97 USA	1959–97 CAN.	1998 USA	1998 CAN.
Contributory Causes (cont.)				
Inadequate belay	124	20	11	2
Poor position	118	15	3	0
Failure to test holds	73	18	2	0
Exposure	55	13	0	0
Failed to follow directions	61	5	1	3
Illness[1]	32	4	0	0
Equipment failure	10	6	0	0
Other[3]	235	79	3	0
Age of Individuals				
Under 15	113	12	4	0
15-20	1158	197	8	0
21-25	1152	225	28	0
26-30	1046	189	29	0
31-35	697	96	21	0
36-50	881	108	23	0
Over 50	140	20	8	0
Unknown	925	577	29	19
Experience Level				
None/Little	1513	280	30	0
Moderate (1 to 3 years)	1354	340	15	0
Experienced	1396	359	53	0
Unknown	1512	384	62	19
Month of Year				
January	187	15	6	0
February	179	40	3	0
March	246	48	6	4
April	338	29	6	0
May	722	48	17	1
June	856	57	25	2
July	942	220	10	5
August	868	137	19	6
September	1059	49	18	5
October	344	30	9	0
November	156	10	4	0
December	62	17	11	0
Unknown	8	0	4	1
Type of Injury/Illness (Data since 1984)				
Fracture	763	146	62	9
Laceration	411	57	36	1
Abrasion	221	39	12	1
Bruise	257	59	17	4
Sprain/strain	189	21	15	0
Concussion	135	14	15	0
Frostbite	86	8	2	0
Hypothermia	105	12	16	0

	1951–97 USA	1959–97 CAN.	1998 USA	1998 CAN.
Type of Injury/Illness (cont.)				
Dislocation	71	8	4	1
Puncture	27	5	3	0
Acute Mountain Sickness	21	0	0	0
HAPE	49	0	2	0
HACE	16	0	1	0
Other[4]	193	31	7	0
None	125	68	9	5

[1]These illnesses/injuries, which led directly to the incident, included: fatigue (4); HAPE (2); and angina.

[2]Because there were so many rappel errors—a category which now includes climbers being lowered to the ground, usually from a sling-shot belay—this year, some of the causes are described here: rappelled off the end of the rope (9!); webbing on anchor "failed" (2 – one knot came undone and one weathered webbing parted); came to end of rappel rope and did not know how to ascend; belayer lowering—rope too short so it passed through the belay device (no knot in end of rope) and climber falls to ground (3); lowered too fast, so climber hit ground (2); figure-of-eight knot to harness came undone when being lowered, so climber hit the ground; rappel rope got stuck so undid harness, then fell 20 feet to ground; and finally, a face-first (Australian or "butterfly") rappeller picked up too much speed and did a face plant (see North Carolina for narrative).

[3]These included: unable to self-arrest (7); handhold or foothold broke off (6); party above dislodged rock; snow bridge collapsed and failed to warn party below; dislodged rock severed climbing rope; "snagged" crampons (2); distraction (2); failed to turn back (3); started late in day, so benighted (4); blown over by wind; and failure to disclose medical condition to guide (see angina in Illness footnote above).

[4]These included: pneumothorax (2); punctured lung, punctured leg (ice ax); internal injuries (when climber fell on belayer); rope burn; paralyzed from waste down.

(Editor's Notes: Data for some categories in this table were published inaccurately, and have been corrected in this cumulative data.

Under the category "other," many of the particular items will have been recorded under a general category. For example, the climber who dislodges a rock that falls on another climber would be coded as Falling Rock/Object, or the climber who has a hand hold come loose and falls would also be coded as Fall On Rock.)

Mountain Rescue Units in North America
(*Denotes team fully certified in technical rock,
snow & ice, and wilderness search)

Alaska
Alaska Mountain Rescue Group POB 241102, Anchorage, Ak 99524
Denali National Park SAR POB 588, Talkeetna, Ak 99676
US Army Alaskan Warfare Training Center #2900, 501 Second Street,
APO, AP 96508-2900

Arizona
Apache Rescue Team POB 107, Nutrioso, AZ 95932
Arizona Department of Public Safety Air Rescue 2615 E. Airlane,
Phoenix, AZ 85035
Grand Canyon National Park Rescue Team POB 129, Grand Canyon,
AZ 86023
**Central Arizona Mountain Rescue Assn/Maricopa County Sheriff's
Office*** POB 4004 Phoenix, AZ 85030
Sedona Fire District Special Operations Team 2860 Southwest Dr.,
Sedona, AZ 86336
Southern Arizona Rescue Assn/Pima County Sheriff's Office*
POB 12892, Tucson, AZ 85732

California
Altadena Mountain Rescue Team* 780 E. Altadena Dr., Altadena, CA 91001
Bay Area Mountain Rescue Team* POB 6384, Stanford, CA 94309
China Lake Mountain Rescue Group* POB 2037, Ridgecrest, CA 93556
Inyo County Sheriff's Posse SAR* Inyo County Sheriff, Bishop, CA 93514
Joshua Tree National Park SAR 74485 National Monument Drive,
Twenty Nine Palms, CA 92277
Los Padres SAR Team* POB 6602, Santa Barbara, CA 93160
Malibu Mountain Rescue Team* POB 222, Malibu, CA 90265
Mono County Sheriff Search and Rescue POB 436, June Lake, CA 93529
Montrose SAR Team* POB 404, Montrose, CA 91021
Riverside Mountain Rescue Unit* POB 5444, Riverside, CA 92517
San Bernardino County So/West Valley SAR* 627 Aspen Way, Upland,
CA 91786
San Diego Mountain Rescue Team* POB 81602, San Diego, CA 92138
San Dimas Mountain Rescue Team* POB 35, San Dimas, CA 91773
Santa Clarita Valley SAR/L.A.S.O.* 23740 Magic Mountain Parkway,
Valencia, CA 91355
Sequoia-Kings Canyon National Park Rescue Team Three Rivers,
CA 93271
Ventura County SAR* 2101 E. Olson Rd, Thousand Oaks, CA 91362
Yosemite National Park Rescue Team POB 577, Yosemite National Park,
CA 95389

Colorado
Alpine Rescue Team* POB 934, Evergreen, CO 80439
Arapahoe Rescue Patrol Box 901, Castle Rock, CO 80104
Colorado Ground SAR 2391 Ash St, Denver, CO 80222
Crested Butte SAR* POB 485, Crested Butte, CO 81224
El Paso County SAR* 3950 Interpark Dr, Colorado Springs, CO 80907
Eldorado Canyon State Park POB B, Eldorado Springs, CO 80025
Garfield SAR POB 1116, Glenwood Springs, CO 81602
Grand County SAR* Box 172, Winter Park, CO 80482
Larimer County SAR* POB 1271, Fort Collins, CO 80522
Mountain Rescue Aspen* 630 W. Main St, Aspen, CO 81611
Park County SAR, CO POB 721, Fairplay, CO 80440
Rocky Mountain National Park Rescue Team Estes Park, CO 80517
Rocky Mountain Rescue Group* POB Y, Boulder, CO 80306
Routt County SAR 911 Yampa Ave/ POB 772837, Steamboat Springs, CO 80477
Summit County Rescue Group* POB 1794, Breckenridge, CO 80424
Vail Mountain Rescue Group* POB 1597, Vail, CO 81658
Western State College Mountain Rescue Team* Western State College Union, Gunnison, CO 81231

Idaho
Bonneville County SAR* 605 N. Capital Ave, Idaho Falls, ID 83402
Idaho Mountain SAR* POB 741, Boise, ID 83701

Maryland
Maryland SAR Group* 5434 Vantage Point Road, Columbia, MD 21044

Montana
Glacier National Park SAR POB 423, Glacier National Park, West Glacier, MT 59936
Northwest Montana Regional SAR Assn. C/O Flat County So, 5 800 S. Main, Kalispell, MT 59901
Western Montana Mountain Rescue Team* University of Montana, University Center, Rm 105, Missoula, MT 59812

New Hampshire
Appalachian Mountain Club Pinham Notch Camp, Gorham, NH 03581
Mountain Rescue Service PO Box 494, North Conway, NH 03860

Nevada
Las Vegas Metro Pd SAR* 2990 N. Rancho, Las Vegas, NV 89130

New Mexico
Albuqueque Mountain Rescue Council* POB 53396, Albuquerque, NM 87153

New York
NY76 SAR Box 876, Guilderland, NY 12084

Oregon
Corvallis Mountain Rescue Unit* POB 116, Corvallis, OR 97339
Eugene Mountain Rescue* POB 10081, Eugene, OR 97401
Hood River Crag Rats Rescue Team* 2126 Tucker Rd, Hood River, OR 97031
Portland Mountain Rescue* POB 1222, Portland, OR 97207

Pennsylvania
Allegheny Mountain Rescue Group* C/O Mercy Hospital, 1400 Locust, Pittsburgh, PA 15219
Wilderness Emergency Strike Team* 11 North Duke Street, Lancaster, PA 17602

Utah
Davis County Sheriff's SAR* POB 618, Farmington, UT 84025
Rocky Mountain Rescue Dogs 3353 S. Main #122, Salt Lake City, UT 84115
Salt Lake County Sheriff's SAR* 3473 E. 7590 S., Salt Lake City, UT 84121
San Juan County Emergency Services POB 9, Monticello, UT 84539
Utah County Sherrif's SAR* POB 330, Provo, UT 84603
Weber County Sheriff's Mountain Rescue* 745 Nancy Dr, Ogden, UT 84403
Zion National Park SAR Springdale, UT 84767

Vermont
Stowe Hazardous Terrain Evacuation* PO Box 291, Stowe, VT 05672

Virginia
Air Force Rescue Coordination Center Suite 101, 205 Dodd Boulevard, Langley AFB, VA 23665

Washington
Bellingham Mountain Rescue Council POB 292, Bellingham, WA 98227
Central Washington Mountain Rescue* POB 2663, Yakima, WA 98907
Everett Mountain Rescue Unit* POB 2566, Everett, WA 98203
Mount Rainier National Park Rescue Team Longmire, WA 98397
North Cascades National Park Rescue Team 728 Ranger Station Rd, Marblemount, WA 98267
Olympic Mountain Rescue* POB 4244, Bremerton, WA 98312
Olympic National Park Rescue Team 600 Park Ave, Port Angeles, WA 9836
Seattle Mountain Rescue* POB 67, Seattle, WA 98111
Skagit Mountain Rescue* POB 2, Mt. Vernon, WA 98273

Tacoma Mountain Rescue* POB 696, Tacoma, WA 98401
Volcano Rescue Team 404 S. Parcel Ave, Yacolt, WA 98675

Wyoming
Grand Teton National Park Rescue Team POB 67, Moose, WY 83012
Park County SAR, WY Park County So, 1131 11th, Cody, WY 82412

Canada
North Shore Rescue Team 165 E. 13th St, North Vancouver, B.C. V7L 2L3
Rocky Mountain House SAR* Bag 5000, RCMP, Rocky Mountain House, Alberta T0M 1T0

MOUNTAIN RESCUE ASSOCIATION
710 Tenth Street, #105
Golden, CO 80401
602-205-4066
Internet: www.mra.org • email: mra@mra.org

Tim Kovacs, President
Central Arizona Mountain Rescue Association &
Maricopa County Sheriff's Mountain Rescue, AZ
602-205-4066
tkovacs@goodnet.com

Rocky Henderson, Vice President
Portland Mountain Rescue, OR
rockyh9@idt.net

Tom Frazer, Secretary
El Paso County SAR, CO
tfrazer@earthlink.net

Jon Inskeep, Member at Large/Treasurer
Sierra Madre SAR, CA
joninskeep@compuserve.com

Rod Knopp, Member at Large
Idaho Mountain Search and Rescue, ID
rsksearch@aol.com